BRAIN STORM

D1452469

BRAIN STORM

a

life

in

pieces

Shelley Kolton, MD

This is a work of nonfiction. However, some names and details have been changed.

Title: Brain Storm by Robin Morgan
Subtitle: A Life in Pieces by Susan Shaffer
Design by Duane Stapp
Text set in Garamond
All photos by Yaz Tulca
Cover photo retouching by Alex Williams
Cover design by Flannery Klette-Kolton

ISBN: 978-0-578-73647-1

Published by FLR Press
568 Broadway Suite #304 New York, NY 10012

*For my three beautiful girls, Flannery, Lili, and Ruthie, for whom
this book was written, and for my extraordinary wife, Susie,
who stayed by me throughout and helped teach me how to love.*

[There is] no such thing as the durable, unique, individual personality… For all I know, every human being has as many personalities as he has interpersonal relations…

—*HENRY STACK SULLIVAN,* American Neo-Freudian psychiatrist and psychoanalyst

―――――――

Being unable to tell your story is a living death, and sometimes a literal one. If no one listens when you say your ex-husband is trying to kill you, if no one believes you when you say you are in pain, if no one hears you when you say help, if you don't dare say help, if you have been trained not to bother people by saying help…

We are our stories; stories that can be both prison and the crowbar to break open the door of that prison. We make stories to save ourselves or to trap ourselves or others—stories that lift us up or smash us against the stone wall of our own limits and fears. Liberation is always in part a story-telling process: breaking stories, breaking silences, making new stories. A free person tells her own story. A valued person lives in a society in which her story has a place.   —*REBECCA SOLNIT, The Mother of All Questions*

Table of Contents

Introduction

_____

This book will not leave you unchanged.

I know. In a half century of working with women in the US feminist movement and the global Women's Movement, I've been fortunate to know four particular women experts in the creativity and plasticity of the human brain—specifically the female human brain. All four being feminists, each in her way has been dedicated to healing wounds inflicted on female human beings by patriarchal culture. All four became friends of mine. All four, as it turned out, had survived extreme childhood abuse and been diagnosed with what was once called multiple personality disorder (MPD) but is now termed dissociative identity disorder (DID).

The remarkable thing is not only the sophistication with which in each woman's case the brain had devised personae as a survival mechanism. (After all, if one's selfhood is violently obliterated in childhood, isn't it a life-affirming response to create a new self—and some extras, just in case?) More, it's that

Introduction

each of these women transformed her suffering into empathy and action to help others. One, a fierce, brilliant activist for the rights of women on welfare, worked for economic justice decades before the term was invented. The second had fled her family to seek sanctuary in convent life but wound up in a psychiatric hospital, vowing that someday she would create a refuge for women driven into psychosis by childhood trauma—which she did, establishing a network of accredited, female-run, supportive halfway houses so that women emerging from mental institutions needn't return to situations responsible for their having been institutionalized in the first place. The third, a distinguished psychologist and academic, has done groundbreaking work on the "institutional betrayal" that compounds personal betrayal, as when women report assault on campuses, or in professional athletics, the military, and other institutions—and are ignored or worse, punished, for reporting the offense. Notice the pattern. Each of these highly intelligent women functioned effectively in the world, even became a pioneer, and a healer of women. The fourth is all those things and *literally* a healer of women: a gynecologist who established the first all-women practice in New York, she is the author of *Brain Storm*—and what's more, she can write.

During the seven years of intense work Dr. Shelley Kolton did with a therapist who understood DID (as not all do), no less than thirty-one alternate personalities or "alters" emerged. Some of these alters required particular therapeutic approaches that didn't work with the other ones. Some had insights into other alters' behaviors, while some were unaware of anything but their own existence. Some recalled fragments of how they came to be, while others could remember nothing. Older alters looked after younger ones. Some of the alters even had alters of their own, which might be a first.

They were mostly female but some were male; as young as a pre-speech infant and as old as the core persona of Kolton herself. Each exhibited great hurt, fear, and in varying degrees, rage. Most exhibited wit. Yes, there is humor in these pages, along with love and loss and the incalculable horror of having been forced to endure ritual sexual abuse as a tiny child.

But Shelley Kolton's "gang," as she and her therapist came to call the alters, didn't exist in a vacuum. Men are diagnosed for antisocial behavior much more frequently than are women, while women by far comprise the majority of people diagnosed with DID. Should that surprise us, given our worldwide, cross-cultural patriarchal society, wherein women and girls are still routinely, violently abused in staggering numbers, as a matter of tradition or religion or custom or "asking for it" or "provoking it" or just "normal life"? How many women are walking around with undiagnosed DID? The voice—*voices*—in this book speak for themselves, but for those other women as well. Yet there are three reasons why Shelley Kolton is unique, even among women with DID, and why *Brain Storm* warrants placement in a larger context.

1) This work is the first to affirm that there *is* a larger context, that *DID is a feminist issue.* Each aspect of the original trauma—from inflicting sexualized torture on mostly girl children and a few "feminized" little boys; on through heavily imposed secrecy and terrifying threats about what will happen if she tells anyone (threats that stalk her, lifelong); to programming her by repeated denial of her memories, conditioning her to question her own experienced reality and (almost) believe she imagined it—all these are tactics of a systemic sadism rooted in the toxic misogyny that brutalizes women and dehumanizes men. The concept that survivors have "false memory syndrome" of their abuse not only blames the victim but is as unscientific

Introduction

and self-serving as Donald Trump's diatribes against "fake news." Both were conceived by the perpetrators to deflect attention from themselves.

2) There have been books and films about women with DID before. But *Brain Storm* is the first work to emerge from that complex *experienced* reality, in detail and with the alters speaking for themselves. The book includes actual emails from the hundreds that Kolton's alters wrote—to the therapist, each other, and Kolton herself. Emails, in their own voices, in real time.

3) The poet Muriel Rukeyser wrote, "What would happen if one woman told the truth about her life? The world would split open." In these pages, Shelley Kolton speaks the truth about a life shattered into thirty-one darkly glittering splinters. Barefoot, she walks us across those jagged edges to the sharpest grief of all—the collision and then integration of the alters, the mourning, the healing of the self. In speaking that truth, she engages what is rarely ever touched on, even by DID-sympathetic psychologists. Kolton's truth risks looking at the cause *and* the effect. What happens to the family of someone struggling with DID? How does her partner cope with these drastic, alien, at times vicious transformations? How do her children deal with this? What happens when she confronts *her* mother, daring to unearth the ultimate betrayal so hideous it has been literally unspeakable? After so many years of work and suffering, can she trust her therapist? Can she trust *herself*? These questions comprise a vast repertoire of pain, demanding that Kolton attempt virtuosity.

How astonishing, then, that this is also a story of *joy*. The story of a life partner whose tenacious love and indomitable integrity somehow held on. The stories of an intrepid therapist who wisely refused to let go; of daughters navigating their own sorrow, anger, and love so as to grow into their own lives and insights. The story of how doing work you love is a blessing, an exoskeleton that braces you upright when your own spine buckles under the weight of what you're carrying, a discipline that defined and drove Kolton to act as a compassionate, skilled physician despite the cyclones raging inside her.

Last, in the largest context of all, this is a story of the human brain. We still know so little about the brain, though the more we learn the more its potential seems wondrous. One of the women I refer to above needed different eyeglass prescriptions for different alters; another's menstrual period abruptly ceased when one of her alters who was male emerged, but then flowed again when a female alter came out or when she returned to her core self. I've witnessed such transformations, grateful to be sufficiently trusted that I was permitted to do so. I have no doubts about the veracity of these women, their alters, and the traumatic and true experiences responsible for their DID. If, as we now know, the brain can devise such physical change as acute pain felt by an amputated "phantom" limb or be able to move a prosthesis via directed impulses, what possibilities might that auger for other ways to focus? What if such powers as evidenced in DID had not been forced into operation by trauma? What if instead they were positive capacities, elegant options a healthy brain might choose and control at will? *There are more things in heaven and earth, Horatio, than are dreamt of in your philosophy.*

So buckle your seatbelt. I repeat: you will not emerge unchanged from *Brain Storm*. It is a harrowing, hallowing experience—and a triumph of the human spirit.

Robin Morgan
May 2020
New York City

My Parts:
The Members of My Inner Gang

Night Writer

Little Girl

Denier

Hate/Raven

Angel

Mary

Twenty

Thirty

Joey

Malcolm

Five

David

Writer

Tommy

Peanut

Scout

Butch/Romeo

Doc

Night

Fuckface

Seven

Aimee

Mom

Speedy

Baby

Little Shelley

Other Seven

Junior

Four

Waiting

Eraser

I

A Perfect Life

My birth augured much of my life—it was fast, and I was eager to start. I did not wait for the doctor, but emerged in an elevator, on a stretcher en route to the delivery room. My mother's doctor, arriving several minutes later, splattered a little blood on his surgical scrubs, smiled at my mom, and told her that they had done a good job together. I started fiercely independent and remained ready for almost anything.

I was born in 1950 on my maternal grandmother's birthday to parents who married young and had children just like all their friends did. They were babies themselves in their early twenties, but they knew how to procreate, even if they did not really know how to parent. My brother Bob came first, and I followed two and a half years later. A mother, father, son, and daughter living in Fresh Meadows, Queens—a perfect nuclear family. Although, of course, we weren't.

Bob and I were primarily accessories—our parents' entrée into normal middle-class life—and secondarily their children who required at least a modicum of care and nurturing, which is all we received. Long before the days of self-cleaning ovens, my mother believed that with the switch turned on, we could raise ourselves and were resilient enough to survive against incredible odds. And so, we did.

I had an idyllic childhood and our home movies proved it. My mother carried me constantly and my father playfully tossed me into the air. While the film may have been grainy, the images of my brother and me chasing each other in our magnificent backyard revealed happy children. With paper hats and blowers everywhere, my birthday parties seemed the best. Movies of trips to the local swimming pool, where my dad encouraged me at the age of two to jump off the high diving board, showed that my parents, to anyone's eyes, were attentive and loving. I went to the local preschool and the teachers knew me as an explorer, an avid climber, and a little one who never cried. In truth, I survived being left by my parents, and although my lack of tears implied a secure and well-adjusted little girl...that was far from the truth.

My mother and father went on lots of weekend jaunts, visiting friends on Long Island, sailing and partying. They traveled to Cuba and frequented Manhattan for dinner and Broadway shows. Bob and I were deposited with my grandparents, my cousin, or the neighbors. We lived next door to the Watkins family—Jack and Virginia and their two daughters. We spent much of our time together because our apartments were attached in a row of single-family homes with plenty of windows and light and space.

My brother and I survived loneliness while my parents climbed the social ladder and landed near the top. My father went to the office every day and worked hard, riding the train to Manhattan, leaving early and returning late. My mother seemed the prototypical anti-feminist not-quite-Stepford wife. Although she gave the appearance of staying home and caring for her children, she did anything but. Her life became quite full, but not of motherhood. Nevertheless, she attested that a woman's place was in the home as she tried to quash my early athletic and intellectual ambitions to be as good and as strong as the boys.

When I turned four years old, we moved to Connecticut, into a suburban house that looked like every other one on the block and like those for miles of blocks around. I loved having my own room and a street I could play on. I rode a bike by five and climbed trees so high that my mother became apoplectic when she found me up there swinging my legs. I remember discovering how much harder it was coming down than going up, but I loved the freedom of being far above the fray, just nature and me.

By the age of seven, I expended enormous energy on my teachers and wanted them to love me. When I called my second-grade teacher by her first name in an attempt to be closer to her, she kept me after school, and I was humiliated and heartbroken. Sad a lot of the time, I believed that my sadness originated with that teacher's anger, but I marched on through elementary school, making many friends and two best ones—Deedee and Robin. From age eight to thirteen, things seemed good, my often-profound sorrow apparently sequestered, although I wanted different, better parents and spent as much of my time as possible at my friends' houses. I did well academically and was athletic enough to play ball with all the boys in the neighborhood and at school. And so, despite my mother's belief to the contrary, I was living proof that girls *could* be as good as boys.

chapter 2

Everyone's Eyes Were Shut

We walked into her office, a small space between the locker rooms and the gym. A Dairy Queen mug sat on her desk, ringed with the brown remains of her morning coffee. A team photo proclaimed "Turn-of-River City Champions, 1963." The blue Victrola on top of the cabinet played "Moon River" and I noticed she'd closed both doors.

We're after the same rainbow's end, waitin' round the bend, my huckleberry friend…

She wrapped me in her arms. I was happy, titillated. She was my basketball coach and I was her star seventh-grade athlete. When she kissed me, my head spun; I was curious, while simultaneously confused and scared. My hormones were raging, and I responded fully. I imitated what she did and within minutes we were on the floor having explosive sex. That was my first orgasm.

I was thirteen and had been searching for a real mother

when Coach Alice lit upon me. She was thirty-two. What followed was a secret relationship that lasted for five years. It looked normal when she coached me in gym class, at practice, and even when she drove me home. We talked for hours in the car, and then again on the phone before I fell asleep. We discussed school and friends, her family and mine, how and when we could be together again, and trips we were hoping to take. After that first encounter, we had sex in her car, in her apartment, in my house, in her office, and anywhere else we could. I was not a big kid. In fact, I was five feet tall and ninety pounds, but I could soar on the basketball court. I figured that my athletic prowess won me the attention of this beloved coach and that sex was part of the package.

I had no clue I was such an easy catch for her. Pedophiles cast their nets wide and pull in whoever is vulnerable. I was not special, I was repeating what I knew, and unconsciously and thoroughly disconnected from the present—I knew sexual abuse well.

I am not sure if I kept this a secret because Alice was my teacher and coach, or because she was a woman, or both, but I knew that I could not tell anyone, and so I compartmentalized that part of my life and did as many typical teenage things as I could when we weren't together. I was neither pretending nor disingenuous as I spent time with my friends, going shopping and talking about boys. I even practiced kissing so that when the boys finally came around, we would all be experts.

When I was fourteen, my parents found letters Alice had written to me expressing her love and recounting the many times we had been together. I had missed a lot of school because of illness and much of what she wrote was about missing me. When I saw my stone-faced mother holding the jewelry box where I'd hidden the love notes, I was so panicked and confused I thought I might throw up. I tried to look as innocent as possible, but I was terrified my parents would discover the truth…and terrified they wouldn't.

My parents deemed Alice's letters inappropriate enough to show the school principal. I was sent to a psychiatrist, as was she. We both went and both lied, saying that our relationship was platonic. The psychiatrists apparently reported that we were "normal." My parents and the school officials all wanted desperately to believe that nothing sexual had happened, and so they did.

They forbade me to see Alice for a few months, but eventually we were able to convince everyone we had a healthy friendship. The relationship was complicated. She was a surrogate mother as well as a lover and pedophile. She bought me presents and took me on ski trips and a weeklong vacation in Florida to stay with her brother and his wife where, despite my being a young teenager, they allowed me to join them in drinking and gambling at jai alai games. Alice and I had special songs and secret ways of communicating, and she was almost always good to me, although what she expected of me sexually was overwhelming. My coach continued molesting me daily throughout junior high and high school. Everyone's eyes were shut.

As I grew older, Alice became more possessive and less tolerant of my "other" life—the normal one. She became overtly angry when my early feminism and college politics took form and were 180 degrees to the left of hers. That was the beginning of the end. I "broke up" with her by the end of freshman year and weirdly, rarely looked back. Several years later, she was booted out of the Connecticut school system for molesting other girls and moved to Florida with a schoolmate of mine. Once, in my early twenties, I traveled to see her and tried to discuss our relationship, but she denied that she had done anything with or to me at all. I was flabbergasted…stunned that she was either lying about our relationship or had forgotten it and what she did to me. I never saw or heard from her again and I learned she died while I was writing this book.

chapter 3

Autonomy

I was thrilled to get away from Connecticut and attend the University of Wisconsin in Madison. I lived in one of the older dorms on campus in a triple room with two other girls and we each bought matching red bedspreads. I was on the top bunk and on top of the world.

College was extraordinary for so many reasons—the antiwar movement, the women's movement, the sexual revolution, marijuana, and the freedom to express my own fierce independence. The 1960s and '70s were a passionate time for self-reflection and action and I wanted to be part of all of it. At eighteen, I was swept up into grown-up issues and I thought everything I believed was right. I returned home during school vacations and argued with my father about the military-industrial complex while trying to convince my mother that my father was a pig and she needed liberating. It all fell on deaf ears, or so I thought. In later years, my dad became quite freethinking, putting women on boards at corporations and consistently treating them with respect. He was the one who pushed me to succeed while my mother continued to disparage my determination.

I liked the image of becoming a professional, of having status and stature, and of prolonging my studies so that I would not need to return to Connecticut. I decided on pre-med, but by the end of the first year, I could not stand the competitiveness in the classroom, so I dropped my science courses and switched to philosophy, Buddhism, and psychology. I was, after all, eighteen and the world was on fire. The National Guard was on campus trying to end a Black student strike. There was turbulence, only exceeded by our passion for the cause—and make no mistake about it, as angry as we all looked protesting, we were pumped up and excited, feeling our collective power. For me, the belief that we could change the course of history was deeply personal. It may have been the first time I felt like I was on the right side of a power struggle, and it was beyond liberating.

Despite my experiences with my coach, I believed in my heart I was a virgin and needed to have sex with a guy. I traveled from Wisconsin to Rhode Island to have my first experience with a dean at Brown who had been my tennis coach at camp. As it so often does, my first time hurt like hell, but it freed me. The enormous pressure from society to have heterosexual sex is something that persists to this day, but back then, there was also a push to have any sex, period. It seemed that everything I did—smoking pot, tripping, having sex with girls and women, boys and men—was exciting and conflict-free for me. I went to Woodstock and became part of history. I felt alive.

Although I flourished in college, this was also when I began to write late at night while I was alone, and my writing was extremely dark. I wrote about exploring my passion for political action and the personal agony motivating it. I was not chronicling my college adventures, but instead my conflicts, my struggles with what to do with my life, my hatred of the Vietnam War, and my disillusionment with government and society. I wrote to ease my pain and it exploded like a steam valve released. By morning, I was fresh and ready for classes and did not remember what I had written. When I looked at my notebooks the next night, I noticed something odd about my handwriting: it changed frequently—in fact, almost daily. Although I wouldn't learn of it until years later, this was the emergence of one of my parts—**Night Writer.**

The idea of over-analysis—to the point of absurdity?

Everything constructed, created, envisioned, internalized—is male?

Therefore everything, rather nothing, is female. Negative. That is impossible.

What is? Hmmm 4 lines 3 questions.

I before E...questions before answers...women and children before men...

Love before marriage...work before play...

———

Maybe this shall mark the beginning of a new form—no attempt at poetry, and hopefully little preoccupation with style, flow, impression + audience. I doubt that I will ever write a sentence without some concern for the unknown readers of the future...

But my political actions of the past are questionable in terms of motivation, and in fact, are questionable in terms of their revolutionary nature + impact. To be sure, I am content with the identity of "revolutionary." But it is still a term, a dream, an ideal. It is also something which I am not...

I express intellectual hostility toward hypocrisy—I suspect that this reflects a rather deep emotional conflict regarding my own hypocrisy.

I wrote this more than forty years before I began this book. Prescient, I suppose.

———

My detour from the pre-med track notwithstanding, I continued to spend each summer in some medically related field, working in hospitals and doing clinical research. Between junior and senior years, I attended a program in Denver, researching and preparing a paper on the psychosomatic responses of asthmatic children. I decided that I really did want to go to medical school and spent my last year in Wisconsin fulfilling all the requirements.

The day my grandfather died was the day Mount Sinai Medical School accepted me. I was ecstatic to have made it, but not at all happy to leave Ruth, an extraordinary woman with whom I was in love, to return to New York and live near my parents again. After my grandfather's funeral, I wrote:

I cannot stop thinking
of the funeral
the bureaucracy of Riverside

the smut of the Jersey Turnpike

the infinity of stone and the

emptiness of life, or memories, or anything

at the cemetery

grandpa's cold skin

the sturgeon, or was it whitefish

and Mildred

good old miserable Aunt Mildred

what a totally fucked-up affair

I hope we have all learned

something

about what never

to do

again.

This was neither extremely dark nor was it written at night. This was the way I felt about being near my family. I was aware that I had taken an oddly and perhaps overly impactful trip to the cemetery, but I brushed that off as normal.

chapter 4

Becoming a Doctor

Returning to New York after college was a shock, and then, it wasn't. I navigated city life and campus life, which was challenging, but I was still on my own, having found a cute studio apartment near Sinai on East 93rd Street between Madison and Park Avenue. I felt honored to be on a path to becoming a doctor. I would soon discover the political left did not solely inhabit the University of Wisconsin campus, but was alive and well in New York City. Although we came from myriad campuses, my new classmates and I had all experienced the same movements and upheavals. We had struggled with the morality of Vietnam, become outraged and terrified by the killings at Kent State, anguished over women's rights, listened to the same counterculture music, and done the same drugs.

My medical school class was one-third women and almost everyone had similar political leanings—every woman was a feminist and every man was avoiding the draft. Our political energy turned to demanding a host of medically relevant and

Becoming a Doctor

socially important advances, including calling for curriculum changes, preventing animal cruelty in experimentation, and pushing the admissions committee for more students of color. Women's rights took center stage and admission and treatment of female students as well as handling of female patients became priority issues.

Medical school rapidly became my new home. I loved it and did not understand at the time why I was so happy during the day and still so dark at night, when I wrote hundreds of pages of poetry and letters filled with pain and struggle addressed to no one in particular. I wrote about feeling split, my handwriting varied from night to night, and I wrote in different voices. I had no idea why. Some of what I wrote began sad and finished uplifted, almost like a good therapy session.

No one else can

Hear me

Or can touch my sadness

So, this page

These words

Are for me

I will hold onto you

And when you feel safe

You can cry

And I will stay by you

This is how it must be

Every love will have its end

Every friendship will need its space

And tomorrow will arrive

On schedule

Untouched by the painful

Night preceding it

The world will look to you

As usual

And you will blink the tears away

Toss aside the pain

Lift your face to the sun and wind

And smile

I was concerned enough to seek out a psychiatrist who was young and analytically trained. It was helpful to have a place to vent and to experience therapy. However, we argued incessantly about the motivations for my political activism. It felt like she was trying to analyze my involvement in the women's movement right out of me. As I began to question what made me tick, I grew depressed and got tangled up in the first of many complicated relationships. I had been with men and women, but mostly I was looking for a mom, and when I fell in love with my professor, it was exhilarating. We had an affair and when she went back to her husband, I bottomed out and had my first adult suicidal thoughts. The sense of loss and grief far exceeded what it should have been, but I was clueless, still believing my childhood had been one of a happy home with perfect parents, and that all I had was an ordinary broken heart.

My nighttime depression arrived on schedule, and normalizing it allowed me to succeed in many ways. I was doing well in medical school, even though it was demanding. I listened to Su Negrin, a lesbian feminist with her own talk show on WBAI radio, late every night and found solace in her personal and political struggles. Toward the end of this time, I was on call and so very sleep-deprived that exhaustion masked all awareness of my mood changes.

I applied to the Albert Einstein College of Medicine OB/GYN residency. My interview with the acting chair of the department (a left-leaning feminist man) went so well that in spite of there being a matching program, he accepted me on the spot. I still had fantasies of returning to Madison, but I was thrilled and at that point, happy to stay in New York. My residency, by all accounts, was fantastic. The program was intense and extremely progressive, and my training was exceptional. I enjoyed being a doctor for women in a program that validated my beliefs that women faced unrelenting discrimination as patients and as physicians. Medicine was a white male-dominated profession then and, to its detriment, remains one despite vast increases in the number of white women and women of color doctors working today.

Looking back, I came to realize that I was emotionally vulnerable, but this was not a dark period for me. An obstetrics and gynecology residency not only allows for but demands a special relationship between attending physicians and residents and nurses. During those long hours on labor and delivery, especially the all-nighters, the staff and I ate together, shared our stories, and supported each other through the joy and stress of delivering babies. The fatigue alone helped to cloud our judgment just enough, and the consequent intimacy formed by spending so much time together led to countless sexual affairs between residents and their professors and the labor and delivery nurses. For anyone looking to act out sexually, this was the place to do it, and so I traded much of my nighttime darkness for sex and the intensity of being on call. I loved the rush of delivering a baby, whether it be an easy catch or a complicated emergency Caesarean section. It was always cosmic; it was always bigger and more important than anything going on in my mind.

I also loved being a doctor. I oozed compassion and was careful not to abuse the power that patients instilled in me. My left-wing politics remained intact and I demanded women be treated with greater respect and humility. OB/GYN was the perfect specialty for me to return power to the powerless, to give women the right to orchestrate their birth experience insomuch as it was possible, and to enable them to participate in their care from a position of knowledge and control.

Political beliefs are never one-dimensional and mine certainly weren't, but there was a fire in me that has lasted to this day. I can't help feeling that a need to rectify old wrongs and soothe old pain motivated some of that fervor and call to action. At the time, I never thought my passion for feminism grew from my own powerlessness as a child. The women's movement was monumental, and certainly not all women were driven by their own personal stories. Or were they? The political summons that resonated for many feminists was not necessarily indicative of abuse, but of years of feeling less than boys as children and far less than men as adults.

chapter 5

Labor and Delivery

I spent four years of residency and many years after raising awareness and calling men on the carpet for being patronizing. Somehow, I alienated only a few along the way, and was thrilled to experience the impact of feminism on the medical community over time. The OB/GYN community was the first group of specialists to embrace new ways of treating patients—like listening to their requests and treating them respectfully—but they still have a long way to go.

After graduating from Mount Sinai, completing my residency, and a brief stint as an assistant professor at Albert Einstein College of Medicine, I went into private practice in Manhattan's Greenwich Village, joining Dr. Marcia Storch, who was iconic in women's medicine. I was high on life and women's healthcare and what I had achieved, but never stopped feeling it was all a sham, that somehow, in some way, I had snuck into the ranks.

Marcia was no longer doing obstetrics or gynecological surgery, so I covered that in consultation with her but was alone in the field, so to speak. For some reason, maybe leftover bravado from my college days, I was unafraid and engaged. A part of me felt I could do anything, and I did.

When a community clinic that was closing asked me to take on all their pregnant patients, I agreed. There were about sixty women, all due within three to four months! I was immediately in a busy practice and delivering about five babies a week. The word got out: in Manhattan, there was a feminist OB/GYN in a women-only practice who delivered babies like a midwife. That person was me! Soon I was approached by one of the finest midwives on the floor at Beth Israel Hospital, who said, "You need me." She was right. Nancy Kraus stayed with me (with one hiatus) for thirty-eight years until she retired in 2019.

Downtown Women OB/GYN Associates was the name we gave the practice in 1990 and although we have changed in many ways, we remain a feminist all-women practice providing high-quality, state-of-the-art care, delivered by women and for women. Over time, our population, providers, and staff have changed, and we have had our share of bumps along the way. Also, some of us older practitioners have learned that feminism has a new face compared to that of the 1980s, and both patients and staff are committed to women's health care in different ways than we once were. Although the conversation about women's politics has shifted over the years, women's health care was once again threatened, this time by Donald J. Trump and the Republican-led mission to eliminate contraceptive and abortion rights in this country.

———

Not all my thoughts about babies were work-related. I had always assumed I would have children one day and being a lesbian did not diminish that wish. Luckily, when I was a chief resident, two women—Sandy and Robin—came to me and asked me to birth their baby. They were one of the first couples in the country to use artificial insemination by a known donor to conceive, and they were in search of a sympathetic obstetrician who might also be a woman and gay. During the remainder of their pregnancy, delivery, and postpartum joy, we grew close. The possibility of having a baby myself became a question of when and not how. Sandy and Robin had created the model, and they were there to help and cheer me on when I decided to get pregnant.

I was already in a relationship with Maureen, a nurse at Albert Einstein who had two children from a straight marriage. We were excited to raise a child together. I asked Jackie and Gail, neighbors and good friends who worked in the fashion industry, to find me a nice gay man who wanted to help me get pregnant with no strings attached. Joey appeared a few months later and turned out to be the perfect donor dad. Trying to conceive back in 1983 had its funny and poignant moments since we were doing it ourselves outside of the medical system. We had temperature charts and that was it—no ovulation kits or apps telling you when to inseminate. It was "Come over tonight!" or Maureen and I went to him, racing through the streets of Manhattan with his sperm in a jelly jar, holding it close to our bodies to keep all the millions warm and alive. We were described by the media as lesbians using turkey basters—a male fantasy and a ridiculous method, and one that I have never known anyone to use.

We conceived our daughter on the fifth try. I loved every aspect of being pregnant. I felt strong and powerful and clearly full of life. As a feminist, I was shocked to discover how primitive and extraordinary preg-

Labor and Delivery

nancy felt. I was so thrilled when my amniocentesis showed that I was having a girl that I raced over to New York University with a pink balloon that I held up in Maureen's classroom. Years later, when I look at pictures of myself on the operating table prepped for a Caesarean section, I recall having flashbacks—this was not the first time I was strapped down naked.

Our daughter was born on July 23, 1984, with ten fingers and ten toes and a head full of dark hair. I did not think life could be sweeter. We named her Flannery at the suggestion of a friend who loved Flannery O'Connor. Life filled up with playdates and birthday parties and friends—new and old—with children of their own. I was still doing obstetrics so it was hectic, and I was totally dependent on our nanny, Linette, who brought Flannery to me on schedule so I could nurse her. Like so many New York City nannies, Linette loved Flannery as her own and was fiercely protective. To this day they remain friends, and Flannery counts on Linette to fill in the emerging blanks of her own history.

—————

The medical practice was growing and booming. We were crazy-busy—patients came from the entire tristate area for care. Being the only all-women's practice in Manhattan helped, because so many women at that time did not want men to be their gynecologists. When Flannery was born, I hired a woman named Debbie Barny as my bookkeeper; she then became my CFO and senior administrator and dear friend and has been with me for thirty-six years. I hired two more midwives and another physician, Beth Shimlock.

After about three years, Beth decided she really did not want to do obstetrics long-term. We had to choose between stopping obstetrics and continuing only surgery and gynecology or parting ways. With Flannery just three years old and me missing a lot of time with her, I decided that I could be happy making the change in the practice. It turned out to be extremely difficult for me to give up delivering babies; it was so much a part of who I was and what I loved doing, but there was another side. I had started to have emotional trouble doing circumcisions, which in New York City is the domain of obstetricians. I hated that baby boys needed to be strapped onto a board for the procedure. It made me feel trapped and worse. I had no idea at the time why this was so difficult for me, but I stopped doing them altogether. A few years later, I stopped doing surgery because cutting into the body became impossible for me as well. I was giving up parts of my doctoring identity without a clue as to why. I'd begin to discover the reasons when Flannery was six years old and I went to the darkest place I have ever known.

chapter 6

An Endless Tunnel

I had affairs with women while I was trying to conceive and after Flannery was born. I acted out sexually and assumed that it was my normal. I was a pro by now, keeping parts of my life separate, all the time thinking I was happy and never questioning my own mental health.

When I was forty years old and she was forty-five, Maureen decided to go to law school and rent an apartment in Newark, New Jersey. That's when things began to unravel, and we could not stop fighting. She dragged me to her therapist so that we could get some help. It only took a few sessions for Carol to convince me that I had some serious problems that needed addressing. I began seeing her several times a week and suffered unrelenting panic attacks. For ten months, I was short of breath and terrified, my resting heart rate was 160, and I had to sequester myself in my office every five to ten minutes so that I could garner the strength to see another patient. Between therapy sessions I wanted to jump out of the nearest window and did not think I would survive until I could get back to Carol.

I was in a tunnel that was loud and dark and endless. I later learned that this noise was the voices of my parts or alters, but at the time I thought it was just an active mind. Ambivalence became my norm and, while I could not yet define it, different personalities were fighting to be heard. This conflict paralyzed me.

I continued to have panic attacks while in therapy until March 1990, when I suffered a massive headache that lasted for many weeks. Two days after my negative CT scan, I had my first flashback and memories poured in and through me like a tsunami—I had no idea how to make sense of them. *Our neighbor, Jack Watkins, naked, standing over me, a terrified tiny girl.* Was I crazy? Were any of these true or was I imagining things? Were they symbolic, as my therapist erroneously came to believe, or did horrible things truly happen to me?

I worked hard to communicate these memories to Carol, but since I was so overwhelmed, I could not speak and so acted them out—or ab-reacted, as it is called in therapy terminology. Carol often came into her office to find me curled in a ball, gagging, choking, or pushing something or someone away. I sought her for comfort and frequently sat trembling near her on the couch. I was quiet and I was petrified. Many of these early recollections came from a time in my life when I was young and prever-bal, and there were no words to express what was happening. I stored the information in my body, and it would be four more years before my older parts gave language to the youngest ones so that I could be heard.

Had my memories consisted of "ordinary" childhood sexual abuse, like, perhaps, the abuse by my coach, I might have begun to heal by artic-ulating them. I might have still been shocked to discover that my perfect childhood had happened differently from my idea of it, but I would have had an easier time believing that something had indeed happened. However, that was not my story, nor could I pretend it was.

By the time I was forty-one years old, my life was becoming dismantled. I now recalled myself as a baby held down and tortured, a little girl raped, a witness to unspeakable acts—a child fighting for her life and remaining silent. I began to draw pictures of my past and of the abuse because I could not put words together. One of the pictures depicted an empty basement with a single light bulb dangling near an eight-rung ladder. A boiler was close by and the ground was uneven, like sand.

My weekly drive to Carol's office in Queens took me along the Brooklyn-Queens Expressway, past the neighborhood in Fresh Meadows where my early memories were set. One day, without any forethought, I turned off the BQE and found our old house—my mother had once given me the address. As I coasted up to the building, I found myself almost in a trance. I walked around the property, transfixed and for some reason, unafraid. As I approached the Watkinses' home next door to ours, there behind the hedge and next to their front door, I saw a grate in the ground. It had a lock that was open and without any hesitation, I pulled up the grate. It was too late in the day and too dark to see in, but luckily, I found a passerby with a book of matches to spare. I climbed down a ladder and into a small basement room with a boiler and a dangling light bulb. The dirt floor crunched under my feet, and when I lit a match, the ladder came into focus. It had eight rungs. *The scene was exactly as I had drawn it.* I was excited and unafraid, thoroughly impressed with my courage. This was my first real clue of the veracity of my memories. I only became terrified later when I truly owned what had happened to me as a child.

An Endless Tunnel

Carol's reaction to my description of this experience was one of surprisingly little concern.

Even so, I had to tell my mother and father. I was not exactly sure how to do it and I had neither the will nor the stomach to confront them directly. I wrote two letters which Maureen agreed to deliver for me. The first acknowledged that I had been depressed for many months and I appreciated my parents' concern. I wrote that something had happened to me when I was young and that I had only recently remembered it. I said that they could choose to read the second letter or not, but if they did, they should be prepared to be shocked and quite likely to find the content impossible to believe. I wrote that I needed them to believe me or that they should not read it. Of course, they asked Maureen for the second letter.

Dear Mom and Dad,
When I was young, I was sexually abused repeatedly and violently. It was not by anyone in the family. I do not want to name the perpetrator because my memories are new, and I don't trust them yet. In time, I will tell you who it was...

It was a long letter in which I was able to lay out my wishes in a way that I never had before. I said what I needed from them was that they be kind and supportive to one another. I did not want to see them yet and did not want to speak with them.

Maureen told me they both wept while reading the second letter and they asked her to tell me that they loved me and would do whatever I needed to get help. Within a few weeks I was able to go to Connecticut to visit them. I walked into the kitchen. No one spoke. We hugged and we cried. It was the only time I can remember my mother and father being *Mom* and *Dad*, protecting me, calming me, loving me. It was a teary re-union until I reiterated that I did not want to name names.

Without missing a beat, my mother said, "Oh, I know who it was—Jack Watkins. He was always a little creepy."

My heart practically blew a hole in my chest when she uttered those words. I had not mentioned where it happened, given no description of the man I saw in my memories. She had no clues, nothing at all to go on, but she named him and in doing so, provided me with the wrenching and heartbreaking truth that she had known something had happened and done nothing to protect me. Years later I would find out exactly how complicit she was.

———————

Over the course of the next decade, I remained in therapy. Despite the copious material I presented to Carol, I was never certain what exactly had happened. Although I read her all my night writing, shared all that I'd drawn, and unconsciously began to use different voices to articulate how trauma affected me at various ages, she did not diagnose my multiplicity, nor did she validate my memories as truths. When I asked, "What do you really think happened to me?" she replied, "We will never really know for sure" or more often, "I don't know." Despite this, sharing my pain released a tremendous amount of internal anguish, which, aided by medication, eventually abated my panic.

What remained was a deep uncertainty about who I was and which of my memories were truths. My recollections of ritual abuse strained my credulity and I spent many years believing that for some deeply pathological reason I was making everything up. I was careful in those early years of recall not to speak with any other abuse survivors or read anything related to the topic until I had satisfactorily remembered my own experience. I knew enough that I did not want to contaminate my recollections and have others tell me I had been influenced by what I read or who I spoke with or what my therapist wanted me to believe.

In fact, Carol was the opposite of those accused of unduly influencing their patients to remember things. She never hypnotized me, and she had read little about ritual abuse. Although I didn't believe my memories, I can honestly say that they were pure and they were mine, and they came from some place deep in my unconscious mind. Advocates of false memory syndrome will disagree, holding to the belief that my recollections were foisted upon me in my vulnerability during psychotherapy and my memories were not my experiences. Why these therapists deny the experience of so many people has never been clear to me, nor were symptoms like mine ever addressed by their theories. My firm belief is that many of them were abusers themselves.

A few years later, doubting every memory I had, I confided in Joan, a friend of a friend. I learned she was raised in a satanic cult and lived with dissociative identity disorder (DID). She accepted what I told her without batting an eye. An intuitive person, she had suspected something was going on with me. I shared my scattered memories and she validated every one of them with a frightening certainty. I wanted someone to say "Nope. That couldn't have happened," and was unprepared for her support.

Joan introduced me to friends and acquaintances who had been the victims of cults. I learned of patterns among the mechanisms used to break people. When Joan and I went to an art exhibit by a woman with a history of terrible abuse, I flipped out. Many of the drawings were exactly like mine, and still, I was not ready to accept my own story. Neither was Carol, so I continued to believe my memories were symbolic and not real. It was all too much for me to process, and so I again distanced myself from other cult survivors and began to doubt Joan's truth, since I could not believe my own. But the possibility of ritual abuse in my case stuck with me and continued to haunt me for years to come.

Carol never quite helped me put things together, no matter how I tried to communicate, but I stayed in treatment with her for fourteen years through my forties as Flannery grew up and my relationship with Maureen dissolved. I was as self-righteous as anyone who has been through a divorce. I was certain that I was the better parent, the better person, and the one who should have custody. It was neither accurate nor fair. It was, without question, a miserable time for all of us, and the misery lasted for several years.

chapter 7

My Own Family

Susie and I met because she wanted to have children. Being a patient of my practice, she already knew I was a lesbian who had conceived my daughter through donor insemination. Susie was a nice Jewish girl (which was new for me) and an accomplished screenwriter. She had a million questions and they were good ones, so we met for coffee. Long story short, we fell in love. It was the year 2000. Although I was as free as a bird, she was in a relationship, but her partner was not enthusiastic about having kids. There were some tense months while she separated, followed by more tense months because I was conscious and then not so conscious of my erratic behavior. I had never been in a relationship that became so intense so quickly and had a future attached to it. I was frightened without knowing it and was desperately "all in" and then "all out" for months, breaking up with Susie and she with me, several times in the first year.

Everyone—my parents, my friends, my brother, and Flannery—thought Susie was fabulous and perfect for me. I could see nothing but her faults, and if she didn't have too many, I made some up. I've never totally understood why Susie got the worst of me in the beginning of our romance, but she obviously got some good as well or she is flat-out nuts. Like ninety-nine percent of women who have been victims of sexual abuse, for me, at some point in all my relationships, intimacy became overwhelming. The association between sexuality and power, pain and control was too strong for me to bear, especially with someone who was powerful in her own right, and so I kept pushing Susie away. I was terrified. She was extremely patient with me and knew of my suspected abuse, which helped her understand what was going on.

My family and friends made an enormous difference. They held firm in their conviction that Susie was the best thing that ever happened to me and if I fucked it up, I'd regret it forever. I heard them and kept their voices in my head during all the tempestuous times. I knew I was hurt and that my take on life was distorted because of my abuse, and so I hung in there. Therapy helped a little, but mostly it was Susie who stuck with me no matter what. Neither of us knew at the time that I had multiple personalities (as Carol had missed the diagnosis entirely), and so my erratic changes in behavior were impossible to comprehend or explain.

In between crazy moments, there were plenty of good times and a lot of excited talk of having children. I had loved being pregnant so much that the thought of denying this experience to someone I loved was impossible. A lot of energy went into figuring out the logistics of how Susie could have a baby. Flannery's bio dad had been perfect, so I lobbied for another known donor, which Susie wanted too. After months of studying, interviewing, and considering different men, we picked a friend, Adam, and were thrilled that he was into the idea. Susie got pregnant after four months and we were ecstatic. We immediately started planning as best we possibly could for the big unknown ahead.

Not long after, we went on a previously planned trip to Italy with my parents, brother, sister-in-law, niece, Flannery, and her friend. On our first night in Tuscany, my brother Bob toasted the family and included our unborn baby. "And here's to Spot!" Susie and I felt celebrated and accepted. It was a fabulous holiday. When we came home, Susie miscarried. She was devastated and I subsequently learned I was cruel to her. As she was hemorrhaging pieces of our two-month-old fetus into the toilet, one of my parts told her: "What, you think you're the first woman in history to miscarry? Get over it."

I learned this years later. The pattern, however, was established: when Susie was hurting, I was a shit.

We persevered and Susie tried to conceive again without success. She was forty-four at the time and the process was draining on all of us, donor included. We decided to adopt and met with a well-known attorney to get the process started. We did well at first, filling out mountains of paperwork, but we stopped abruptly when asked to make a glossy brochure to "sell" ourselves to women wishing to place their babies with adoptive families. We were both turned off and overwhelmed by the whole thing and by then, I was advocating for an egg donor pregnancy. So off we went to IVFNJ, a respected fertility center in New Jersey that advertised a large bank of egg donors. After a thorough intake and a meeting with the donor coordinator, the doctor, and the billing department, we were set. It took four hours. We chose an egg donor with a good medical history who was of Irish descent and a scholar-athlete. They told us she looked like Winona Ryder, but of course, who really knew? All we had was a baby picture, a poor-quality Xerox of a happy three-year-old with big, engaging eyes. We had far more information about our sperm donor. He was a Jewish philosophy student with a healthy family history whose favorite book was Plato's *Allegory of the Cave*. This blew us away because it is also Susie's favorite book and we knew unequivocally that this was the universe telling us he was the one. He sounded intelligent and sensitive on his audiotape and the picture of him as a little boy was precious. Now we had to get Susie's cycle synced with the egg donor's cycle, which required painful daily shots that I reluctantly administered and Susie took like a trooper.

When Susie was ready, we decided we would only transfer two embryos because we did not want to reduce the number once they implanted. We did *not* want triplets. Susie conceived on her first transfer and at the six-week check, both embryos had implanted. Twins! We were over the moon—giddy and terrified all at once. Her early pregnancy was good—she looked great, and yes, she had that glow. But in her last trimester, she developed a case of PUPPP (pruritic urticarial papules and plaques of pregnancy) or in other words, an unbearably itchy rash head to toe. She was miserable and up all night every night for weeks. She was treated with steroids, which gave her diabetes, and she was suffering. She was induced at 36½ weeks and after many hours of labor on August 5, 2003, she had a Caesarean section. She was delivered by my partners, Audrey and Suzanne, who sweated through a blackout at NYU Hospital. On the tenth floor, without electricity. In the summer. No lights, no air conditioning, no elevator. A very feeble generator. They were fantastic.

The girls were beautiful. Flannery was there taking pictures. We were one big happy family. Lili, named after Susie's grandmother Lilian, was born first, and Ruthie, named after my grandmother Ruth, came one minute later. They were pink and healthy and came home with us after three days.

My former nanny, Linette, who had come back to help us, dubbed Lili "Chili Pepper" because she reacted to everything around her and was harder to soothe. Ruthie was a quiet and curious baby, and easy to pacify despite Lili's crying. I felt that because I had parented Flannery, I could calm Lili better than Susie could, even though she was the one nursing both babies at the same time. Years later, when I was able to hear about it, I was devastated to learn that I often got angry with Lili, shaking her when she screamed, quite the opposite of calming her.

Flannery was nineteen when the girls were born. She was at New York University and navigating her own issues. She felt excluded from the new family as if she'd lost me to them. She had begun acting out in high school, not really knowing that as a child she too had been the victim of my angry outbursts. We were close, but she wondered if we had been too close, and if my lack of boundaries had significantly impacted her. In high school she had become anorectic and by college she was drinking and taking drugs in excess. When the girls were born, she felt that she had to get her act together for them, but it took her years of working on herself to arrive there. She went to culinary school after college and became an amazing chef. Today she is happier, healthier, and successful, but there are still pieces of her childhood she doesn't remember well. Our guess is that she dissociated herself in response to my abuse and lack of boundaries.

Unfortunately, the gaps in our history of Flannery's years growing up will need filling in over time. My memories are only good ones—I adored her and never imagined I was anything but loving and protective. As I came to understand my history and degree of dissociation, I came to know that things were not always rosy.

chapter 8

Finally Yael

As life went on, my relationship with Susie deteriorated, and a few years after Ruthie and Lili were born, we began to see Lida, a couples therapist, to help us make things at home tolerable. Since I had no awareness of much of my upsetting behavior, I had no understanding of Susie's frustration and anger and I sought to blame her for everything. We fought constantly and the kids heard it all. They acted out, which made us fight more, and the cycle continued. I wanted and needed additional time on the weekends for myself, and Susie tried to give me as much as possible, but I continued to be drawn into the family dynamic because my family also grounded me.

Lida became acutely aware that I needed to deal with my trauma and suggested a new technique, EMDR—eye movement desensitization and reprocessing—but she couldn't perform it with me because she was already our couples therapist. Practically frantic, I agreed to meet her colleague, Yael Sank, who specialized in caring for trauma patients.

Finally Yael

I did not really want to meet with another therapist and retell my story, only to hear what I already thought happened to me, but my pain and desperation to keep my family together propelled me into Yael's office. She greeted me on that first day wearing a white stretchy headband. I disliked her at once. How could I work with someone who looked so pretty and perky and straight?

She knew of my abuse and she knew that it was horrific. I had not gone into a lot of detail, but she felt confident we could work together. Several months into therapy, and after she accumulated a lot of information from me, she explained EMDR. In the process, I would be tapped, buzzed, or beeped using a device designed specifically for this purpose, providing a redirection while remembering my past. Yael placed a small vibrating buzzer in each of my hands and instructed me first to imagine my safe place filled with beloved people or pets. I was acclimating to the setup when Yael turned on the buzzing machine. Instantly overcome by abject terror, I hurled the buzzers back at her.

Yael was calm during that horrible panic attack, although taken aback by my dramatic response. She suggested we not use the buzzers quite yet. She also thought I should give her even more background, so we could target the trauma more effectively. I decided that to speed things up, I would show her my artwork, read her some of my night writing, and give her more information about my history, tentatively using the words "ritual abuse." It was a desperate move, filled with blind trust and effected only by the escalating darkness of my dread and misery. My artwork was explicit and graphic— images of children being assaulted and faces of cruel people—and my writing was deeply personal, containing page after page of panic and despair.

Unlike Carol, Yael believed me.

A few weeks into my treatment, Yael arrived at her office with hundreds of pages printed from the Internet, documenting the existence of ritual abuse, what Randy and Pamela Perskin Noblitt in their seminal book, *Ritual Abuse in the Twenty-First Century*, define as "abuse or maltreatment that occurs in a ceremonial or circumscribed manner and where the abuse causes trauma-genic dissociation and/or establishes or reinforces control over dissociated states already in existence." This definition was expanded in 2018 in the journal article "Psychiatric Impact of Organized and Ritual Child Sexual Abuse," which says ritual abuse is "often rooted in the child's own family" and "occurs when a religious, political, or spiritual authority uses its position of power and the sovereignty to interpret the respective belief system to manipulate and dominate its followers."[1]

Yael pointed out the similarities between the current psychological research and what I had shared with her in our earlier sessions. She was careful not to introduce any added information that I might incorporate into my memory. After years of seeking help, the certainty with which she studied and sought to understand my pain and her openness to explore all the details was such a relief to me that I experienced a lightness of spirit I had never known. My brain was quiet and at the same time noisier than ever. I had a million questions and a sense of hope; I felt that maybe, just maybe, I had landed in the right office with the right person at the right time and I might get better.

After a few more sessions, as this foundation of trust developed, my parts—what I called my inner gang—began to appear.

---

1 Johanna Schröder, Susanne Nick, Hertha Richter-Appelt, and Peer Briken, "Psychiatric Impact of Organized and Ritual Child Sexual Abuse: Cross-Sectional Findings from Individuals Who Report Being Victimized," *International Journal of Environmental Research and Public Health* 15, no. 11 (2018): 2417.

Chapter 9

My Gang Speaks

———

The first time it happened, I sat only a few feet away from Yael in her tiny office, a position that usually made me feel safe, but this time I was about to explode.

"Shelley, what's going on?"

I couldn't squelch my intense agitation. "I feel like I'm going to jump out a window!"

"You're safe here, and there are no windows. Why are you so panicked?"

I couldn't respond and my head felt weird, like something was crawling up the back of my hair. I spaced out and disconnected from my body. For a moment, it was a pleasant kind of high. Then, I watched incredulously as a little girl appeared in my place on the chair.

"Hi," she said in her tiny voice.

Very softly, Yael replied, "Hi."

I sat there. My legs pulled up under me. I was small.

"Who are you? Do you have a name?"

My Gang Speaks

"Little Girl."

As I spoke the words, I saw myself, sitting on a daybed in a sunny room on the second floor of the two-story house next door to my childhood home in Fresh Meadows. I could hear footsteps and knew Jack Watkins was about to come through the door. He was a big, ugly bald man dressed in khaki shorts and a graying white T-shirt with armpit stains. I was three. He was ageless to me then, but likely in his early thirties. In the memory, I knew what was about to happen, and I came to understand it meant this was not my first encounter with Jack, although it was the first memory to return to me. He dropped his shorts, made me lay down, and put his penis in my mouth. He thrust while I choked in silence. He eventually finished and pulled up his pants. He cleaned me up and carried me downstairs to his living room.

Yael was visibly nauseated as I stammered out my recollections as best I could, still feeling like I was only three years old. When I'd finished, she asked, "Are you okay?"

I couldn't answer.

She waited patiently. Our session had ended, but she now sat across from a three-year-old child who had to go back to work—patients to see and medical procedures to perform—before she picked up her kids from afterschool care.

Yael finally asked, "Is Shelley here?"

I tried to break into Little Girl's space because I knew I had to grow up. My head was stuffed with thoughts about what I had heard—*me*. I was somehow there but not there. I was unsure if I remembered everything Little Girl had said, but I knew I had to answer Yael.

"Yes."

"Hi. Are you Shelley?"

I nodded. Still spacey. Voices rumbled in my head and I was aware for the first time that there seemed to be others, perhaps many others, speaking within me, *living* inside me.

"Do you remember my meeting Little Girl?"

I nodded again.

"Can you come back and speak to me, so I know that you are safe to go?"

"I'm here. I'm Shelley." This took supreme effort. I wanted to stay small. I wanted Yael to comfort me forever—I felt safe with her—but I could sense myself coming back to the present, back into my body and my adult personhood.

"I hear you and would like Little Girl to come back and see me at the next session. Is that okay?"

"Sure," I said, without knowing how in the world I could make that happen.

Yael repeated that our time was up, I needed to go back to work and see patients. She asked again if I could do that and I told her I could.

And I did.

I was a little dizzy and fascinated by the whole experience as I went back to my office and sat there for a moment, ruminating about what had happened. And then I worked; I saw patients, I provided comfort and diagnoses, I wrote notes. When I had finished, I picked up my children and went home to Susie, who was preparing dinner for our family.

I spent the next few months alternating between fear and despair, and every so often, complete normalcy. I thought a lot about Little Girl and she indeed came back to speak with Yael. I could not get a handle on why the pain was so searing and the despair so profound. The moments of normalcy were equally confusing and reinforced my denial that anything had happened. Susie was my rock then and has remained so to this day, but to say that our relationship was smooth, especially during this time, would be a gross misrepresentation. It was not easy, and I was not easy. I lived from therapy session to therapy session, hoping for yet fearing the breakthrough that might cure me.

———————

Four months after my first meeting with Yael, she looked at me intently at the beginning of a session, her eyes kind and concerned, and said, "You have DID—multiple personality disorder."

"Seriously? You're kidding, right?"

"No. I'm not kidding. You have parts who are separate from you. Little Girl has shared her memories with me and in my process of observation, I see that you are dissociated from her. That means you have a part that is outside your consciousness. And there are others—"

Again, "You're kidding!"

She wasn't. "Do you remember what Little Girl told me?"

"Some of it, I think. I remember Jack and I remember being terrified."

Yael shared her understanding with me. She told me that another part, a teenage boy with a distinct voice, whose name was unknown, had spoken with her.

I had no recollection of this, but as I processed what Yael said, my response was the opposite of what one might expect—I felt tremendous relief! I was happy. My pain had a name and hopefully that meant that I could get well. I was a doctor, and I knew well that the first step toward treatment is a diagnosis. I was determined to approach DID the way I had most things in my life—medical school, marriage, mothering, and advocating for women's health care—with passion and an intensity of purpose.

I liked putting a label to what I was experiencing and was eager yet anxious to tell Susie what Yael thought. I anticipated the same immediate response of "You're kidding!" but instead Susie needed no time to accept this information and replied, "There have been *so* many times I've said 'I don't know which Shelley is going to walk through that door after work.'" She added, almost with relief, "Of course."

Flannery, who was twenty-three at the time, agreed. "Yeah, that makes sense, totally."

My brother Bob was the only other person I told very early on. "Really? I'm sorry. I can see that." He, of course, began to wonder if anything happened to him.

I had second thoughts about liking the diagnosis. What did Susie and Flannery and Bob mean? *What* makes sense? Did I have other parts who talked to them, parts unknown to me they'd met before?

II

chapter 10

The Work to Be Well

———

Over the course of the next ten years, thirty-one members of my gang—alters—emerged, each with their own voice, their own story, their own set of needs, and their own way of healing. When I was open to them, they all clamored for attention. The noise in my head was often at a crescendo—the decibel level of an elementary school cafeteria and equally unpleasant. I heard distinct voices, but they were out of control and for a long time I didn't seem to have authority over any of them.

I knew they had a lot to say but I learned to wait until I was safe in Yael's office and she could hear and document everything. I existed between sessions as best I could and tried to hold down my panic. I was no longer intrigued, as I had been when Yael first diagnosed me—in fact, I hated my diagnosis and denied it repeatedly, but gradually...very gradually...I sought peace with my parts and they with me. I'd come to recognize each one.

The Work to Be Well

My therapy took off at breakneck speed although the finish line was never in sight. Together, Yael and I struggled to find a way to recall and then process each memory without my being re-traumatized, as if the abuse was happening all over again. There did not seem to be a way for me to remember except by marching straight through the memories themselves. It was brutal. I thought recounting my story with Yael would be inherently therapeutic, but it wasn't. This part of the process did not allow the part who held the memory to resolve any of its emotional content; it did not allow me to feel what I had felt and to unburden the grief that went with the terror. That would happen later.

Yael could never be there as much as I needed her to be, which was always. Sometimes I left her office feeling drained and spent, yet with a sense of closure. At other times it seemed as if nothing had resolved, and I was stuck in the memory—not unlike having a nightmare and being unable to shake it despite the knowledge that it was only a dream. Leaving a session without closure was a new kind of torture. I wrote in my journal:

Cannot shake it. Memory is so clear it feels like yesterday + I am still feeling aftereffects. This feels like therapy w/Carol. Bringing it up, reliving it, and then having nowhere to put it. It goes from something we are dealing with to something I am dealing with, living with. I hate everyone. No one can really save me, it's too late. No one cares that much anyway. It's a big world—I won't really be missed that much. Abandoned again. Don't want to abandon my own kids but don't feel strong enough to go on. Doesn't anyone get that? Doesn't anyone get that I need a break, relief, I need it all to be over. I feel like I already died on that table so dying a second time will be easier. Fuck you every-

one. Fuck all of you who keep pushing me to remember. Why do I want to remember this shit anymore? It is beyond horrible. It is beyond imaginable. It is mine, all mine + it is all fucking real.

The noise in my head began to seep into my day-to-day functioning. My dissociated existence pre-therapy had a whole lot of appeal. I forgot how destructive my behavior was, and how panicked I'd been, looking for help with my symptoms. My past, even then, seemed rosy. I knew I couldn't go back but moving forward was so daunting that I often felt paralyzed. I was shocked by how difficult the work to be well had become.

This may be a good thing, but I feel like I am coming unglued. All day I was wandering in and out of my mind, in + out of my alters, in + out of any focused person in charge. I could not stick, or stay, or hold the person long enough, before someone else popped out. Don't think it was noticed at work tho' I felt it. By the time I got home, I was in full-blown crazy, raging angry one minute, weeping sad overwhelmed + small the next. I terrified the kids twice today. Once in the morning, once tonight. They are both pushing my buttons, but especially Lili + she is getting the lion's share of my anger. And she gathered herself to come + apologize before I could even catch my breath. And she is 4. It feels like the walls are cracking and coming down. The noise is deafening. I feel agonizing pain, overriding panic + complete despair all in the same moment. I am dreading tomorrow's session with Yael + it cannot come fast enough. I still do not have enough time to do the memory work, process the day-to-day stuff in my life, talk with Yael about the process itself so that the time in between sessions is not spent either recovering from one session or dreading the next. If five hours a week of therapy can't do that, what will? 6? 8? 10? I am a bottomless pit of toxic waste, waiting to have enough holes punched into me so that it can all escape, so that it can ooze out + go back into the earth + then deeper. So, is all this good? Must I be shattered, yet again, so that some rebuilding, reconfiguring can occur? I thought we could maybe have a détente with everyone inside—I was not expecting a nuclear attack. And nowhere near enough drugs this week to keep me numb.

Couples therapy became a disaster as well. I began to dissociate during our sessions, and the stress of hearing why Susie was so angry made me escape into another world—I went completely silent. For me, it was like stopping in the middle of a fire to analyze the flames. I wrote a letter to Lida, Yael, and Joe (Susie's therapist):

> *This is an excruciating time for me, as you all know from your own perspectives. I am filled with shame and grief, waiting for bursts of terror, and not really trusting anyone…I am doing all I can to function, to go to work, to keep my children feeling safe, to work on my marriage, and to show up for therapy, which often leaves me feeling worse than when I walked in….*
>
> *I have little or no self-esteem and a dearth of self-love right now. My memories have left me feeling completely and utterly unloved and untouchable, and anything that comes my way in session which reinforces that feeling sinks me deeper into a hole that I cannot climb out of. For me to even have to think this through and write about it feels supremely burdensome and unfair…*
>
> *So, I am going to be really clear here. I have times when things are manageable. I have times when things are not, and when I am there,*

I am hanging on by the tiniest thread. I am feeling pulled into a thousand more directions than I already lived in, and more importantly, I am not feeling truly protected by any of you...

I need to keep my marriage intact, but I cannot be expected to do couples work that ends up being more upsetting than helpful. I know that I pushed for more sessions together, but sadly, I cannot handle the stress of them. I feel that Susie needs and deserves whatever support she can get from Joe and you, Lida. Maybe together you can ease her own terror about losing me.

My job, at this point, is to not lose myself and to survive this journey and perhaps find some joy at the end. Right now, I cannot see any light at all.

I am not sure where to go from here, but I needed to react, to let you all know that this is where I live.

Because of this, we stopped couples therapy shortly thereafter, which helped to free me from the stress of hearing Susie rage about everything I did. I asked her, at Yael's urging, for more alone time—time away from the kids—and she tried her best to give it to me. It was not easy for her to manage them when Lili was having a dysregulated or reactive day, but here and there I had time to restore and prepare for the work week. I read, wrote, played my bass, and paused to just *be*. When I wasn't panicking about being alone, it was heavenly.

One of the hardest things, if not the hardest, to learn about panic and despair is that the symptoms usually abate if you can survive them long enough to see the other side. But they recur, repeatedly and often unpredictably, during the process of healing, and when you feel the weight of either, you cannot see the exit light.

The Work to Be Well

When I re-read my journal today, I wondered how I could possibly still be alive. And then I realized—there are good days too. Maybe even great ones. Today, I had a long shower, three hours alone, time to read, 1 orgasm, time to play the "Moonlight Sonata" on the piano after a 20-year drought + some time to just do nothing. The kids were good, I was nice to Suze, I took all my drugs as ordered by my oh so smart therapist, and I feel kind of restored. I will try hard to not expect this to last + thus feel like a failure when I am down + dark again. But for now, I will try to enjoy it.

It does not feel possible to identify my splitting when I am responding to life's stresses. In therapy, I expect to dissociate + when I do—and I do because it is safe to—I am often remembering some trauma + so the split is expected. When I am writing and alone and also safe, I can dissociate + although I may not know it at the time, I can recognize it after the fact. I was shocked re-reading my journal—and just since October. My despair, hopelessness, rage, confusion is not accessible to me today. And so, if provoked, in life, I split—I do not see it, recognize it, know that it is happening. I know the first goal will be to re-associate, integrate, whatever we call it, in therapy, but that seems so easy compared to integrating in life since I am clueless about splitting. At any rate, I feel pretty good, and a little sad, knowing what lies ahead. I do believe I am in able, trustworthy + loving hands with Yael, but I also know that I will not always feel that. My certainty the other night that I could not trust her was painfully disconcerting. So it's good, I guess, to have it in writing, here, now, today, that we will be ok.

I tried to get a handle on dissociation and how I could get well. Intellectually, I was stymied. I may be a smart person, but I didn't have the answers about how DID worked and how to undo it. I received some help from an unexpected source.

chapter 11

Little Girl

———

Little Girl, my first part to show up in Yael's office, was three years old, but she remembered abuse from the age of one. She had a distinct small voice and a facial expression that Yael came to recognize. Little Girl knew a lot about what had happened to me and once she felt safe, she had plenty to say. She had also emerged with my previous therapist, Carol, who sadly had not seen her as a separate part, instead treating her as if she were symbolic. Little Girl was anything *but* symbolic. She had curly brown hair and blue eyes and wore a white dress. She loved Yael from the beginning and trusted her implicitly. My belief is that the brain creates an image of a part and certainly of one who is as significant as Little Girl. However it works, it was always soothing to have an image of her that was very much alive.

For some reason, Little Girl was also easy for me to believe and so I did not expend enormous energy objecting to her existence. Her first memories were of Jack's sexual abuse and these were clear and credible. After all, at this point in my adult life my mother had already named him as the perpetrator when I had told her about the cruelty I suffered. Jack trained Little Girl to be silent, to not cry when molested, and to never talk about what happened. This was all training for the ritual abuse that came soon after. A dissociative state makes all of this possible for the victim, and ideal for the perpetrators. It allows them to have power and control over a child who forgets or suppresses what happened.

I sent Yael hundreds of letters and emails over the years. The language in a lot of my writing was more sophisticated than the part who was writing it. I can only surmise that an older part was helping since I often have no recollection of the process.

Little Girl wrote:

I want to feel safe. I am sad + terrified at the same time. This is when I feel like I will explode and cannot really separate the emotions. It feels like the noise of being little + so alone + I can't cry so I am holding it all in but it's kind of slipping out, or I'm slipping + I can't hold it in anymore but also if I cry I may die + that is why I'm so scared to let go. Nobody really gets this state I'm in. It is really noisy + scary + emotional + confusing. Confusing cause I'm not sure what to do when I'm in it cause it is paralyzing—usually helps to talk with Yael but not today. No one else can really make all the pain go away, disappear, change my brain, erase my history, hold me until there are no more tears left and no more scary people.

Although I had frequent flashbacks during the day and terrible dreams at night, I never had the full picture or a complete memory until I was with Yael in the safety of a session. Little Girl told Yael that she was in a basement-like space and there were other people around besides Jack. She could not see their faces but could hear them and knew that there were at least three others. Many of my memories were not complete in the first or even second go-round. Flashbacks were exactly that—they were startling moments in time without a beginning or end.

Parts of memories became whole after many abreactions with Yael or verbal (and sometimes physical) expression of previously repressed experiences. In bursts, I learned that each abusive ritual began with a car ride to somewhere and ended with a car ride home. The drive there was always terrifying because I knew where we were going. I began to dissociate as soon as I saw Jack and usually did not return to reality until I got up the next morning.

As my memories became more complete, the rituals revealed were increasingly complicated and devastating. Most of the time, I was in the center of a group of ten or fifteen people, strapped down on a table while everyone chanted around me. Sometimes they had sticks and prodded and poked me, while moving rapidly in a circle. At other times they threatened me with knives or blindfolded me while they penetrated me anally. I recalled playing with a baby who was subsequently murdered for crying too much.

Little Girl was held under water on many occasions and was naturally afraid of drowning. Jack forced himself into her mouth until she couldn't breathe, escalating her terror. Each instance of cruelty was coupled with yelling—admonishments that I was being punished for talking, or crying, or telling someone what happened to me. My abusers told me I was disgusting and deserved each act of cruelty. Nothing was further from the truth, of course, but they made me feel crazy and messed with my reality.

Little Girl

This was also how they introduced and sustained my shame.

At times, my tormentors consisted of a group of men and women. They were always naked under some sort of robes, and the sexual energy was intense and perverted; yet the more terrified I was, the more aroused I became and so began the hideous coupling of the two sensations. This was their ultimate power play, used to control me and to make me behave. When their actions became more sexual, I called upon other parts to handle things, just as I did when their actions became more violent. I'd learn over time that some of these parts were allies, while others were as evil as my tormentors.

chapter 12

Denier and More

My experiences of therapy with Carol and Yael were vastly different. With Yael, I processed memories in a new way. The first time around, I was a witness, watching as I was tortured physically and sexually, but I was not re-experiencing the memories as I later did with Yael, because I did not believe what had happened to me and I had not defined the parts of myself that were holding each of those memories. Those parts never healed with Carol as they had not been recognized and each needed to resolve in their own way, in their own voice, at their own pace. The parts themselves had to be acknowledged individually, because they had their own memories, their own experiences, and their own autonomy within my behavior.

When I began with Yael, I had no control of my alters because they had dissociated from my consciousness. And so, when I needed to function as a doctor and take care of patients, my little ones wanted me to take care of them instead, and they revolted by creating noise and havoc in my brain. The result was panic, like any child would experience if abandoned, and the interruption at work was horrendous. I was glad to have a job to go to, because at times it succeeded in drawing me away from my pain as I was struggling to get through each day without exposing my internal chaos to my patients. When Yael first delivered her diagnosis, she told me to take six months off—that I needed time to remember and to process—but I could not afford to and did not do that. I think that had I had free time between therapy sessions, I might have gone even madder than I was already.

Yael's office was one floor above mine in the same building. She was not in Manhattan every day, but she was always available by phone or email. Amazingly, I never ran into her in the building, either coming or going, although I always wished I would. I felt, in the early years, like I might die without her, and knowing she was close by was a big advantage. The convenience was, of course, unmatched. I was never late for a session, never stuck in traffic or on a subway, and a few times over the years was able to pop in with short notice when I needed a safe place to explode.

Before I could integrate my parts, I had to know them all individually as they clamored to be heard. In fact, most of the time, my head was exploding with different voices, making certain demands and pulling me back into memories. Each alter had to trust I would not abandon them, and I had to trust Yael would not abandon me. I emailed and texted her almost daily, sometimes with insights and sometimes to make contact because I was panicking, seriously depressed, or suicidal. Sometimes I wrote to tell Yael that things were wonderful, and it was important that she know that as well.

We talked about our emails, about the hugs I received as I left or the physical comfort I received when I was in extreme pain. I felt safe and she felt comfortable, but we discussed it in cycles, whenever I worried that she might pull away before I was ready or that my anger might scare her off for good. Little Girl, with the help of an older part, often spoke for all the young parts and wrote:

> *Is there no one out there who really gets this? Do I have to be alone again—without a grown-up, without love, without protection, without anyone seeing what's happening? Maybe if I'm really really lucky, I won't wake up. Fuck everyone.*

As Little Girl's accounts of the rituals became more complicated and vivid, my conviction that they occurred diminished, despite Yael's continued belief in their reality. I had an active denial system in place, and so for every memory I had a part named **Denier**. He was adamant that none of the abuse ever happened. He believed I had fantasized these improbable scenes for a reason that was never clear.

How could we survive without denial? Denial is what enabled me to live my life and it is also what slowed my healing to a pace that was manageable. Denier has been an ever-present part of my gang and still exists today. He has had to work hard to keep me from believing anything ever happened to me. Before my memories and therapy with Yael, this protected me and allowed me to live as fully as possible, but once my memories started flooding in, Denier became an opposing force, and a difficult one at that. He could be active for a minute, or for days or weeks. He was steadfast in his belief that nothing bad except Coach Alice ever happened to me, that I made it all up or dreamed it or saw it in a movie—anything other than the truth. He was challenged when anyone believed my story and triggered when someone did not.

Denier and More

Denier was so strong because the cult conditioned me to distrust my experiences. This was done by systematically pairing my abuse with phrases such as "No one will ever believe you" and "You are making this all up." I re-heard these commands frequently whenever I recollected the abuse. This programming became an obstacle to my recovery until Yael figured out what was going on.

I wrote in my journal:

Denier is alive and well inside me...sometimes I do not believe I was abused at all. I might have a terrifying abreacting session that leaves me disconnected, spaced out, and despairing and then the next day tell Yael that I didn't believe anything really happened. Sometimes, her incredulous look is funny enough that we both have to smile and recognize that Denier was doing his job really well. In all seriousness, it was traumatic enough to experience my memories, without the added trauma of struggling with reality.

My dissociative behavior, as reported to me by Susie, went a long way toward disempowering Denier. When I believed my wife, which I always did, and realized that I must indeed have DID, I deduced that real things must have happened to make me that way, and so, within a month's time, six or seven more alters appeared.

During one session with Yael, I was unable to speak. She gave me a pad and pencil. Although right-handed, I took the pencil in my left hand and identified myself. I was an angry part, too furious and too frightened to speak yet ready to free myself from the gang.

When Yael asked me who I was, I wrote: **Hate.**

We watched with some fascination as I scripted out things that happened to me, things designed to take me apart—being trapped in a box, being shocked with electricity, witnessing a cat killed—all moments that felt like hours, all leaving me full of rage.

Raven was the part of Hate who could speak. I didn't meet him until later. He would turn out to be one of my greatest protectors yet he also caused me the most grief. I was never conscious of my rage until Raven emerged and dominated the gang. After many years, I learned to feel my rage and express it, staying conscious the whole time. I did not appreciate this rage, but at least I was aware of it, remembered it, and could apologize after the fact. This was new.

Raven remained a dissociated part for another five years, present without my awareness, wreaking havoc for my kids and driving Susie into a living hell. What I experienced as garden-variety crankiness emerged as seething rage, much of it misdirected at home. Raven was nasty, critical, judgmental, and brutally mean-spirited. He was most identified with my abusers, being a part who learned what to expect by allying with those who were hurting him.

During the time Yael and I worked together, ever more parts appeared. There was **Angel**, who floated above me when I was in the worst pain but was seldom there. **Mary**, my overeating part, loved chocolate and was enormous and a little tough to control. **Twenty** was the part of me that went to college, had a lot of sex, and smoked a lot of weed. And **Thirty** was thirty years old—grown-up Twenty who was still looking for a mother.

The more alters who appear, the lonelier I get. I am so overwhelmed with the diagnosis of DID, and with the work that has to be done, I can barely breathe...

Denier and More

*My fuse is too short, my anger is out, not even under the surface.
I feel homicidal, suicidal + plain miserable. I have lost any inter-
est or intrigue to figure out the puzzle which is my mind. I would
like some peace + quiet. Just a day to smell the roses, watch the
sunset, laugh with my kids, walk along the river—without noise,
without voices clamoring, without judgment, analysis, thought.*

Again and again, there I was, half hearing my parts speak, thinking this
was too crazy and not believing any of it. It would be repetitive, to say the
least, to record every time I doubted the credibility of my stories because
I doubted them constantly. For every memory, there was disbelief, yet the
images kept coming in glimpses and flashes, bits of a scene that might not
fully emerge for weeks or months. Often, the memory was the same: a
group of people chanting and threatening, sacrificing something living—
an animal, a baby, an adult human being.

If this all sounds far-fetched, well, it was. How could I believe such depravity and such systematic and deliberate abuse? How could these people
have had so much access to me? Where were my parents? Why was I out
in the middle of the night as a toddler with strange people? Where did this
all occur and why were no bodies found? How could this happen without
someone knowing? Was my mind making all this stuff up? Had this been
staged but somehow perceived by me as real? And why could I smell and
feel the memories as if they had just occurred?

These are all fair questions that I needed to answer before I could finally believe what happened to me. The answers came over time, in fits and
starts, but enough to finally satisfy me. The depravity question was the
easiest because we have seen it on a large scale in places like Nazi Germa-
ny, Bosnia, and Somalia, and in a variety of ways every time we turn on

the news. As I'd later learn, the perpetrators had access to me because my parents were either away and I was in their care or because my mother was somehow involved. ˋ

Where the victims came from and what happened to their bodies was one of the most difficult, if not *the* most difficult, thing to understand and to believe. As we see in the news daily, nefarious things happen and the evidence disappears. Clever people use their intellect and connections. Cult activity has been found to be associated with both organized crime and government-funded research on mind control.[2] In this context, it is easier to comprehend the underground mechanisms of the cult. Jack worked for the United States government and was photographed with several presidents. He had a prestigious job which was part of his appeal to my parents. Although my father became angry at Jack's manipulative personality and distorted sense of power while we were still neighbors, my mother remained in his thrall, and in fact, as I discovered in later memories, had an affair with him.

---

2 James Randall Noblitt and Pamela Perskin Noblitt, *Cult and Ritual Abuse: Narratives, Evidence, and Healing Approaches, 3rd edition* (Santa Barbara, CA: Praeger, 2014).

chapter 13

Being Heard

In October 2007, within a few weeks of learning my DID diagnosis, in preparation for an appearance on the MacNeil/Lehrer Report where I was scheduled to speak about menopause and hormone replacement therapy, I attended a conference on menopause at the Roosevelt Hotel in Manhattan, presented by the Yale University OB/GYN department. It was a subject I knew a lot about, but I wanted to be as up-to-date as possible on the current research. During the lectures, I found it next to impossible to concentrate. My mind wandered so much that to keep focused I started to write on one of the hotel notepads we'd each been given.

That night, at the end of the first day of the conference, when I went back to look at my notes, I was stunned. This is what I found, in childish handwriting:

> *I am going to be killed today and I need to say good-bye to my mother and tell her I love her I am three*

Being Heard

years old and I am nice but they don't want me to grow up they are afraid I will talk even though I promised to be quiet they are going to drown me first and they are going to stab me a lot of times in my chest until I am all chopped up + then they will take all of the pieces + bury them in the grave with the dead lady + all the bugs + worms + I won't have to feel them this time cause I'll be dead goodbye.

The following day at the conference I felt pretty much okay. I did some writing during the lectures, but was not dissociating and was totally conscious. I wrote how confusing it was to have gone from suicidal the previous day to normal and mentally healthy the next. In fact, I felt mellow and relaxed and could not access the part of my brain that had attended the conference only the day before and written those childish words. I wondered about my mind and all its occupants and hoped that I would be able to keep them straight.

Upon returning to the hotel for the final conference day, I wrote again in childish handwriting:

Can somebody help me please?
The man is loud
and scary and is going
to kill me. I don't
know how old I am
but I know that I
can't take care of
everyone anymore

I am way too little and

scared. They are holding

me down now there are

3 of them + 1 of me +

they have my arms + legs

and they have already

killed the cat by smashing

it against the wall

until the head was all

crushed and bloody + dead

I finished the conference with the latest information about menopause, but even more insight into my brain, my gang, and my moods. Back home, memories flooded my mind by day and night, so much so that I stopped sleeping. I stopped eating. Susie said I was "spaced out." I began to journal and to email Yael, who encouraged me to write more and often, suggesting that it might help to recognize and decipher the "talking heads" that I complained about. At times, work became unbearable because of my panic, but it also grounded me, allowing me to accomplish something and distract myself. I saw my patients and made a conscious effort to shut out the noise in my head and maintain some degree of empathy. After every patient meeting, I returned to my office so I could breathe. Breathe deeply. It didn't fully abolish the panic but it made time pass with less pain until my next session with Yael.

I was beyond exhausted, on my way to losing thirty pounds, and taking painkillers to self-medicate. My patients and my work partners could tell something was up. I explained what I was going through to my partners. They urged me to do whatever it was I needed to do. I wrote emails to friends with whom I had not been able to talk for months and told them my diagnosis. They all responded with love and encouragement which convinced me, at least for a moment, that my life was worth fighting for, although many times over the next several years I would lose sight of that.

———————

Halloween 2007 was approaching, and my panic soared. This, along with several other holidays, had been a day of torture for me. New York City takes Halloween very seriously and the parade of masks and ghosts and satanic paraphernalia was too much for me to bear. My girls wanted to be ghoulish and I couldn't tell them "No, that would make Doctor Mommy crazy," so they triggered me as well. It initiated an unrelenting fear that the ritual perpetrators were returning for me and no one could convince me that the abuse was over.

This drove me to Google Jack Watkins. I discovered that he had died the day before at the age of ninety-one—peacefully in a nursing home, with his girlfriend nearby. My intrigue at this synchronicity was outdone only by my fear—he had four daughters, two of whom I knew from growing up in Queens. Since they were around when the abuse occurred and I had learned that cults were often family-run enterprises, I Googled each woman. They all worked with children! I considered writing to them but was reluctant to open that door.

Halloween passed and my spirits improved almost immediately but the news of Jack's death became a reminder that he'd been alive at all, he was real but I'd lost the opportunity to confront him. I believed I would never know the truth of what happened to me.

————

Little Girl had not been able to cope with all the abuse on her own and needed some older boys to help her. As I spoke about this in therapy with Yael, my next part came out—a five-year-old boy who remembered doing unspeakable things to another child. It was difficult for him to talk and to recount what had happened.

"What is your name?" Yael asked.

He wrote it on a piece of paper: **Joey**.

"How old are you?"

He held up five fingers.

"I'm glad you're here, Joey. Can you talk to me?"

He shook his head.

I saw him in his dungarees and a striped T-shirt. His hair was short and he was cute.

He looked around the room to make sure he was safe.

When he spotted some toys on Yael's bookcase, he tentatively pulled down a box of plastic soldiers. He sat on the floor and Yael joined him.

Joey made a circle of soldiers and placed one in the center. He then made two of the soldiers smash the one in the center. He said nothing as Yael watched in fascination.

Then he spoke. It was heartbreaking. He spoke to Yael in fragmented, panicked sentences, saying that he had helped the bad people kill a little girl. His hand had held the knife and the little girl died after he stabbed and stabbed. Joey sat still, stoic.

Being Heard

"You know that the bad people were holding your hand, Joey, and you couldn't have stopped them?"

Joey was not buying it. As it would turn out, he did not relinquish responsibility for years, for hundreds of sessions, until he was able to see how little and helpless he had been. Joey wrote:

I have time now + all I want to do is figure out how to kill myself. Suze said to call Yael but I don't want to talk. I don't want to talk to anyone. Nobody. Never ever. They don't get it all of them. They don't know when we are all jumbled up how awful it is + like we're really gonna listen to some grown-up who wasn't even there when it all happened. No way. Can't trust anyone. Just be quiet + do as you're told + maybe just maybe they will let us live let us go home.

I am Joey + I am trying to keep it together here but little girl is so panicked she is freaking out cause they keep doing more things to her and she hates it when they put her under the water + hold her there + she's cold and she can't breathe + a cock's in her mouth + she wants to die + throw up + kill somebody but she can't so she floats away + then it's my turn cause everyone knows how mad I can get + they hope I will kill one of the bad people but I only kill a little baby + she's screaming + squirming + trying to get free + I am so mad that she is screaming + they tell me that I can make it stop I can make her stop and she is not good like little girl cause she is too noisy + so she has to be killed + so I help to shut her up + it feels good when she finally stops screaming + I don't really care that she's dead cause at least it's quiet now + little girl is ok + soon we can go home + watch TV + forget about everything that happened. For a while anyway. I think maybe they will all have to kill me too to get some peace.

I would like to kill myself right now. But not with a knife which is way too messy even though the stabbing part feels good but no I would have to kill me a different way like maybe a gun or jumping so I know for sure I would be dead. Can anyone out there hear me? It's really dark + lonely in here alone.

In addition to Joey, other boys appeared—all of them five years old. There was **Malcolm**, who had long, curly, reddish-brown hair and brown eyes, and wore jeans and a T-shirt, like Joey. **Five** held everyone's pain and was disembodied so I never saw him. He was also mute and so **David**—who was a voice with no body—spoke for him. The boys had experienced their own atrocities of violence demanded by the cult. Joey and Malcolm recounted sexual acts they'd performed on the women in the group—mostly little hands going into grown-up vaginas. Sometimes they were forced to watch as women lowered themselves onto Little Girl's face as another way of suffocating her. The four boys did their best to protect Little Girl but became victims themselves.

Joey was the most animated of the four, and during our sessions he was able to remember many of the details of our abuse. What he was not able to do for several years was to *feel* the pain, both physical and emotional, that he was enduring. That task was left to Five who, because he was often mute, was not able to talk about his pain, but it was palpable in our sessions. He often curled up into a ball or shook uncontrollably while remembering things that were done to him. He was able to answer questions by nodding or shaking his head and identified himself by holding up five fingers. When Five could no longer contain his pain, David would emerge to give Five a voice.

Like so many other times, this was a dark period in therapy. The torment

Being Heard

David described was unbearable and relentless, and I did not believe that I could survive both remembering the abuse and feeling the emotions that resulted. My body hurt so much that I wanted to die, but as I was to discover a million times over, the will to survive was indeed extraordinary, and so I did.

———

Meanwhile, things at home were unraveling fast. Our girls were now almost five years old. There was more fighting and noise and we were struggling with Lili, who was a reactive and hypersensory kid. She had tantrums that included kicking and biting, which provoked me. Although I was aware that our home life was made more difficult by Lili's challenges, I did not know that I was contributing to her outbursts with my own. I mistook Susie's protective behavior toward Lili as *over*protective and resented my wife's belief that she was the more responsible and reliable parent. Susie's awareness of my DID had not made my nastiness any easier for her to tolerate, and she did not fully understand at that time that I had no recollection of my dissociated behavior and that I was not really hearing her when she told me to stop screaming.

I reserved my energy and much of my love for therapy and Yael. Our work together became more intense. We increased our sessions to six hours weekly. Other young parts were emerging, and they needed her steadfast love and attention. More than anything, I needed her trust and her boundaries. I wrote more emails as I searched for answers and begged for a connection to life, waiting for a response from her that would carry me to our next session. This was a time of crisis for me, and I leaned heavily upon Yael's strength, honesty, and love.

Therapy rarely consisted solely of conversation. I screamed and cried out a lot because I had to relive many of the atrocities I experienced before I could purge them. Sacrifices were the most difficult, even more than the physical pain I endured. It could take a whole hour to recount one horrible event, largely because words could never fully convey the brutalities. I had one memory of being in a grave with an old woman, bugs and worms crawling all over me. The story emerged in bits and pieces because I could not fully recount it through my terror and disgust.

Another memory found me with needles under my toenails and yet another had me in a green box with my hands and feet connected somehow to electricity. The horrors were endless.

Yael needed to stay strong, although some of my memories brought her to tears. For the first time in my then fifty-seven years, her obvious horror and hatred of the people who hurt me allowed me to believe I had a legitimate reason to be in pain. Much like the stages of grief, there are stages of recovery from trauma. For me, despair came first and tears came last, because during much of my abuse I had been threatened with death if I cried or made any noise. I went to all kinds of places in my head to get away from my pain, but I did so silently.

All victims of any kind of abuse, especially children, learn to be quiet, both during and after the abuse, and to dissociate, for there is no one with whom they can unburden their grief. The biggest part of recovery lies in being heard, and then being told repeatedly that you did not cause this to happen, you were not responsible, *you are innocent*. Yael must have said these words to me a million times over the years until eventually and finally I was able to believe her.

chapter 14

Disturbance in the Field

Yael and I began to read everything we could get our hands on. Books by survivors of ritual abuse, about survivors, for survivors. Books and articles for therapists and for the families of people with DID. Every book, even the ones that were poorly written, was helpful in some way. There were patterns that were hauntingly similar and suggestions for healing that were tremendously helpful. Yael and I went from our work one-on-one to an anonymous network of patients and therapists who shared their stories. It was comforting and informative.

The dismal news was that my healing would take years, and the process would seem as daunting as the abuse itself. This was akin to having a nightmare in which you are tortured and must go to sleep night after night, knowing you will have the same nightmare. I continued to write, which comforted me. **Writer** did the writing for me. Like Night Writer, Writer was a part who knew all the other parts, and hence really knew the whole story, but only wrote for the parts when they were ready to speak.

Disturbance in the Field

Frustration ran high, with my growing acceptance that some part of me knew everything that I was trying to remember but was allowing me to go through the agonizing process of teasing out each memory, one by one, with all the full horror and terror to go with it. Many things that Yael and I read reinforced that therapy should be guided by what the patient wanted and needed. This was obviously not a traditional approach and we both had to learn to trust each other's instincts. I knew I had to "go back" and "be in the memory" and as much as Yael hated witnessing a reenactment of my abuse, she often felt that she had to follow my lead. When she said "Enough!" I tried to listen and return to the present. It was a dance we mastered over the years—but one that changed and evolved and got discussed repeatedly.

Several times, after Yael went to a conference, read a book, or met with a colleague, she became excited and energized about learning a different method of processing the trauma—a way that might not be so painful. We would discuss and then agree to try it. Usually, I was skeptical and she was enthusiastic. More often than not, I hated the change. What we learned was that many DID patients worked as we did, and many did not. I found that each of my parts also had a preferred method of therapy. **Tommy**, my adolescent boy, for example, wanted hypnosis and EMDR and did not want to reenact anything traumatic. Each part had to find their own way and Yael and I had to figure out what was best for each of them.

———

The noise in my head was constant and I couldn't find peace. Things at home were still coming apart. Susie and I fought in front of the girls, which made them act out. I regularly exploded in anger but didn't recall doing so until I was told about it years later. When Susie tried to describe my behavior, I disconnected and didn't believe her. Meanwhile, therapy with Yael was excruciating and yet a sanctuary in its way. In the safety and support of her office, my parts emerged without my control and with my limited awareness. Within a month's time, Yael and I met new alters: **Peanut**, **Scout**, **Butch/Romeo**, and later **Doc**.

Peanut came first and journaled:

Now my head is quiet but too quiet. Someone is here + we're not talking. She is hopeless + sad + full of self-loathing. She can't see or feel or touch the good stuff. She is 14 + she belongs to Alice. She is completely split off from all the others + can never ever talk to them. Her name is Peanut. She doesn't want to go on, but she does for some reason. She doesn't want to be with Alice but she goes with her every day and does what she is supposed to do. She hates it though + hates herself + knows that she is not normal but no one else knows that. There is nothing more disgusting right now than the thought of a little girl lost in a woman's body, doing things that little girls don't do. I am empty—too empty to even throw up. disconnected. Can someone talk to me?

I resisted Peanut's existence for a long time because I needed to feel like being with Alice, my gym teacher and coach, was my choice. I felt that it had nothing to do with my earlier abuse, which I was still denying as well. I also had the bravado and self-righteousness of a teenager who believed that I controlled everything, and in so doing, felt guilty and loathsome about this relationship. It took many years for me to understand that Alice molested me and that I did not seduce her. Blaming the victim was never so true as it was when it came to how I treated myself.

Because I had always remembered Alice, I did not have to recover memories about our time together. However, I did have to recover my feelings, those locked away in my dissociative mind for many years. What I initially recalled was all the good stuff and there was plenty of it. I needed someone to pay attention to me, take care of me, and love me; Alice did all of those things. She also had sex with me, which defined the relationship as molestation and neither nurturing nor okay. She was a classic pedophile and I was a classic victim. I had already been abused and had a mother who was not at all present, so I was ripe for the picking. She never had to force me to seek her out, and in a way, I had been custom-made for her. Because we had sex almost every day, I had become a sex addict by the age of thirteen.

Peanut is my only young alter who remembered everything without suppressing memories. She is fourteen and the little girl whom Alice molested. Peanut is also my most complicated part, because she participated "willingly" in the relationship with Alice. I was vulnerable because of my early abuse, but I nevertheless remained conscious throughout much of my time with her. I knew I was living a split life and had to keep my relationship with Alice a secret from everyone. I became adept at moving between my normal adolescent world, full of school, friends, football games, dates, sleepovers, and spin the bottle, on the one hand, and my sex-addicted secret life with Alice. I also learned over the course of time that I needed to lie to her about my friendships with other adults whom I knew she would find threatening. Still, in a significant way, Alice was a loving adult who ironically and remarkably contributed to my self-esteem. She made me feel taken care of and important to someone for the first time in my life.

Disturbance in the Field

I was not aware until recently how overwhelmed and frightened I was during the entire relationship and especially while we were having sex. I was conscious of how anxious I was that someone might catch us, so much so that I created an alter named Scout whose main job was to keep us safe from anyone finding us while we were having sex. Scout was my lookout and carried all the terror I experienced by hiding. Scout watched for my parents if Alice and I were at my house or watched out for anyone if we were having sex in her car, which we did often. Scout was responsible for keeping everything about Alice hidden from my friends, who never suspected anything sexual was going on.

I wrote in my journal in November 2008:

When she would touch me, I began to believe that I had found that love that I was so desperately seeking. I felt the hole getting filled up and I wanted more + more + then some. I was like a starved child who had just been fed + I was ravenous. I went from depressed to obsessed + I could not get enough but I knew to keep trying.

Being rescued became sexual as being abused had become sexual. Everything became jumbled + yet I continued to carefully organize my life, keeping everything + everyone in its proper place, and separate. I had no trouble organizing the greatest hoax + deception imaginable. I could have as easily been off murdering people, robbing banks—but instead I was prostituting myself. And so my neediness + my sadness + my loneliness not only got buried, but it became disdainful—for it had driven me right smack into this woman's body, where I lay feeling simultaneously aroused and disgusting. Satisfied + guilty. Smart + stupid. Old + young. And confused.

Disturbance in the Field

There was only one time when we were almost "discovered," by two gym teachers who came to the house when Alice was there. They called her to the back lawn and we both came out to meet them. I heard Alice deny that anything was going on, and tell them to leave her alone. She was furious. I was both terrified and emboldened by her authority and self-righteousness. I was also very much aware at the time that I wanted to be caught. And saved.

When I was nineteen and in Madison, both Alice and a very close friend of mine who was a priest came to visit at the exact same time. We went out to dinner and I brought a friend for support. Alice was furious, jealous, and nasty. Father Bob was quiet and observant. He had known me since I was 14. After dinner I went back to my room and called him. He picked up the phone and said, "I understand everything now. It's ok." That marked a huge turning point in my life—the secret was out, and also I could see that I had outgrown Alice and now had the courage to leave her. And so I did. Just like that. Of course, I fell more deeply in love with Bob than I already had been and two years later he left the priesthood.

The addictive sex with Alice had resulted in promiscuous behavior with boys my own age and with men. The first time I had intercourse, as mentioned earlier, I was nineteen, and it was with a married man who was a dean at an Ivy League college and my summer tennis coach. My modus was to have secret affairs with unavailable men and women, and this behavior lasted well into my forties. If there was no secrecy, there was no arousal; this evolved directly from Alice and from my original abuse.

My sexual acting out was a critical thing for me to understand and to stop. Thinking about sex was the best way to deal with my feelings of abandonment, but after thoughts came action, and I acted out sexually until I was fifty and then stopped when I met Susie—or, I should say, stopped *after* I met Susie. I was attracted to her because she was a hot brilliant Jewish woman who was not available, at least at first. I did not know that she was going to become the love of my life and my rock.

Then there was Yael. Beautiful, smart, funny, compassionate, and seriously straight. It seemed as if she had turned herself inside out to take care of me and there is little that's more appealing than a nurturing woman. I had always been attracted to unavailable people and so this made sense to me, but it was terribly distracting. Amid agonizing and heartbreaking memories, there was a part who continued to obsess about taking my therapist to bed. Most of me knew that I didn't really want to sleep with Yael, and all of me knew that she didn't want to sleep with me—but that did not quash the obsession. Once I let this part out and named it—Butch/Romeo—I had to start understanding it and change its behavior. This was a part who had been out and functioning for many years and it seemed near impossible to either accept it or rein it in.

Butch/Romeo was a two-person part, always operating in tandem. Butch was a lesbian attracted to other lesbians; Romeo was bisexual attracted to straight women, straight men, and unavailable lesbians. Together they were incredibly seductive. They were especially adept at taking straight women to bed and helping them deal with the tumult of their questionable sexuality. Yael was straight, unavailable, and my therapist, which made her a triple bonanza. Although I was able to suppress most of my wishes to seduce her, Butch/Romeo was always around to misinterpret a tender moment, a hug, or the exchange of personal information.

While my little ones desperately needed physical comfort and reassurance, Butch/Romeo needed release from their obsession, something that

Disturbance in the Field

took many years to work through. It contributed to a lot of confusion, but Yael dealt with it head-on, with honesty and sweetness and humor. By understanding the root of my sexual addiction, I began to resolve conflict presented by Butch/Romeo because I trusted Yael completely and because, without trust, there could be no healing.

Email to Yael

If I think about having sex with you then I don't have to think about anything else, especially what happened to me when I was young. As soon as I remember and remind myself of what happened, my obsession lifts. It feels like staying consciously in the past protects me from obsessing in the present, but that is not a practical way to live.

Sorry to write this and not hold onto the thought until Tuesday, but I guess that is the nature of obsessions, after all. And since it was already in the room today, I don't really feel like I was or am off the hook in dealing with this face to face. Deep down, Little Girl does just want you to take care of me. I can't say the same for the adult me (Romeo? Butch?) yet.

When do things lighten up here, anyway?

chapter 15

Doc

Before my diagnosis, there were many clues that something was wrong. After my first memories, I knew, at the least, that I had PTSD from some early abuse. What I experienced personally, more than anything else, was shame about past behavior—often an angry response—that seemed perfectly fine at the time but was horrifying to hear about weeks or even years later. When I learned about this behavior it felt so out of character and I did not know how to interpret it or understand where it really came from. I did not see myself as an angry person, but Raven had been present without my knowing. This occurred both at home and at work, where I felt on some level that it was safe enough to split, and was likely why my business partners, especially Audrey, who had been on the receiving end of this angry part, told me they weren't at all surprised with my diagnosis of DID.

In retrospect, I was able to function as well as I did because I had a part named Doc who was separate and highly functional.

Doc

After my diagnosis, although work grounded me during the day, plenty of things still triggered me. It did not escape me that gynecology was both an odd and a perfect choice of specialty for someone with my history of abuse. During my training, I treated women and children who had been raped, and in practice, almost one-third of my patients had a history of molestation or sexual abuse or rape. Always aware of my history with my coach, I was especially compassionate with these patients and never triggered until I started believing something terrible had happened to me before Alice. That's when my system started falling apart. Doc stopped being an independent and highly functioning alter, becoming regularly vulnerable to intrusions from patients' problems. What had been compassion turned to grief and sometimes panic.

EMAIL TO YAEL

I spent an hour with a patient today. She is a therapist. Her forty-year-old son was a heroin addict and blew his brains out with a shotgun. First, he shot his wife but did not kill her. My patient made a 5-inch-thick scrapbook starting with his birth, a book honoring his life. She had to show me every page, every entry, every email he wrote, including the one when he said goodbye.

I didn't start the day well before that and I am not holding up so well now. It feels like the black veil has come back down over me and little light is apparent. I am trying to be there for everyone, but I am slipping again.

Not exactly sure what is going on when this happens, but it never feels like I can "figure" my way out of it.

I found it increasingly difficult to work. I was afraid to see old patients who knew me well and might suspect something was up. I was afraid to see new patients because I needed Doc to be intact and s/he wasn't. I was afraid I would make mistakes if a young part showed up, or afraid I would get angry at my partners or staff and say something cruel or over-the-top critical. Also, at this point, I was performing transvaginal ultrasounds much of the time. The procedure required placing a long phallic probe in the patient's vagina and reading the screen in a darkened room. I became acutely aware of what a bad place this could be for my angry or abusive parts to come out, and at the same time, it was triggering for the assaulted parts of me.

I began to see transgender patients and became known in the community as a physician who was comfortable with them and sympathetic to their special needs. I was fond of them, and whether they were female to male or male to female, they all shared a certain sweetness, coupled with tremendous courage. For me, they were living the life externally that I often felt I was living internally, which was gender confusion because of my male parts. I saw a patient once who was a female-to-male transgender person. He had a perfectly trimmed beard, short hair, and was of somewhat small stature. His voice was midrange. He was adorable. When I went to examine him and do a sonogram because he was bleeding, his body was covered with hair as any man's would be, but when I sat down to do my exam, I found he had a vagina. When I scanned him, he had a uterus and ovaries, too. I found myself jealous of his maleness. I realized how often I'd wanted to be a man (or maybe had been) in my life.

Although I loved seeing these patients and still do, they did trigger me at times and made me wonder if my gender was in question along with the rest of my psyche. That sent me into yet another tailspin.

Doc

Spiritually on empty. I hate to sound any alarms but seriously, what is so bad about suicide? I will not be here to regret it or to see the suffering that it causes. selfish I know, but true. I changed clothes 4 times this morning. couldn't figure out who I was, what gender, how old, or even what city I was in. would you like me to define torment?

chapter 16

As Needed for Pain

From early on in therapy, Yael was aware that I was medicating my emotional pain with Fioricet, Tylenol with Codeine, and Xanax. She also knew that years before I began therapy with her, I had been hospitalized to get off prescription drugs. She was quite clear with me that I needed to get off them again as part of my ultimate healing. No other therapist in the past seemed to care about my medications or to have the guts to bug me about my addiction. I had become uneasy myself about the drugs—nervous about getting the prescriptions, finding myself without enough, wondering when the pharmacist was going to blow the whistle, switching drugstores. Medication relieved me in the moment, yet provoked a tremendous amount of anxiety, and I was ready to tackle this with Yael's help. As part of my recovery, I knew I needed to taper the drugs, unlike the first time when I stopped cold turkey and spent a week in the hospital. Thinking about stopping drugs, I wrote:

As Needed for Pain

. . . too terrified to go to sleep. Can't turn off the light. Can't lie down. Can't let Suze hold me cause it feels like I'm being held down. Took Xanax. Took Fioricet + Vicodin. Took Ambien. Don't know what a doctor will tell me to take instead of all this shit but I need something to calm me down. I am jumping out of my skin. Just wrote Yael ½ hour ago + said I was ok. Then got into bed + started twitching. I wish I never had to go to sleep, especially at night. Dark, cold nights—that is when it all happens. The rituals, the noise, the craziness, the torture, the knives, the sacrifices, the terror. It is all at night, it is always cold. I am often without boundaries, without anything to make me feel secure, intact, held together. I feel free-floating, falling, all the time, like I am being dropped from nowhere to nowhere. I am little, I cannot speak, I do not know safety. I am desperate for someone to catch me, swaddle me, hold me tight, keep me warm, protect me, keep me safe, away from the bad people.

. . . I am feeling some primal terror that I imagine is pre-death but is complete + utter lack of physical safety.

. . . need to be grounded, to know that it was over. But it didn't happen. It kept repeating. They came back for more. I waited every night, every day, every minute. I was never safe.

I knew I needed medical help, but my internist, Sharon, was one of my closest friends, and she was unaware that I had started overusing drugs again. So, I took a deep breath and told her, and then arranged to see her partner, who was familiar with drug addiction and getting clean. He was a handsome gay doctor named Stephen, who did not really get DID at all. In fact, he wondered about the veracity of my memories, so it was not the easiest of first meetings. After an hour and a half, his perspective and his understanding grew and together we made a plan. I would begin to taper my drugs over a period of three weeks and then he would prescribe a medication called Suboxone to take in place of my usual drugs. It was like methadone treatment but superior in many ways.

My competitive fire was sparked and I was determined to tame this beast. It was April of 2008, almost one year after I met Yael, and I was conquering one of my demons. I had already tapered my drugs down to almost nothing in the three weeks before I took the first dose of Suboxone on a Friday afternoon in Stephen's office so he could observe me for a few hours. Then I went home and took a second dose. Then I got sick. I was so ill for the next forty-eight hours that I wanted to die and thought I might. I was having a terrible reaction to the drug and vomited violently every twenty minutes for the next two days. Susie was on the phone with Stephen and Yael, making contingency plans to admit me to the hospital, but I was adamant about staying at home. Unfortunately, this siege took a toll on my mind as well.

Because I was not merely sick—this treatment was my decision—I took responsibility for everything that was happening to me. Hence, feeling punished was my overwhelming state of mind. I truly felt that I had brought this on, that in some twisted way I deserved it, and worse, that my punishment was not over.

While I dozed between trips to the toilet with the most wrenching heaving I have ever experienced, when I was awake I was jumpy, terrified, and talking to myself or my selves. I often forgot where I was or what was happening. I shot out of bed, carried by my wobbly legs, as I sped to the bathroom where, in heartbreaking terror, I vomited from the deepest place within me. I felt pathetic and pitiable. I thought I might die and hoped I would. The detox was like an exorcism, but I was desperate to succeed for my family and for Yael, and I had an unnamed part—probably Tommy—who was decidedly determined with me.

I survived the weekend…*just.*

Email to Yael

There is no question that I will need EMDR to get over the weekend. It was horrible in every way, physically, emotionally, and spiritually. I asked Stephen this morning if he had devised this scheme so that I would never go near drugs again. He could only laugh sadly.

At any rate, I am off everything. I cannot take the new drug and I have not taken the old. I am in some suspended state of not knowing what will come next (that seems usual for me) and longing for some peace in my body. Interspersed with forty trips to vomit were flashbacks and splitting and body pain that was reminiscent of my worst abreactions. I must have looked like an exorcism was occurring, only I fear that I still have a shitload of more stuff in me. As I dozed dazed for two days and two nights, I was terribly reactive to any street noise, movement, light, the simplest sounds of my kids' breathing. Everything awakened me with terror, and I had several conversations with no one in particular. In other words, I was both whacked-out and not so much. This seems to be who I am.

Email from Yael

I sure hope it was an exorcism…it's been expelled…let's hope. I am glad for your sake that you didn't end up in the hospital, although I don't know how you managed that…the worst is over.

We don't know what's coming next. We just know that it keeps moving you closer to health. Your determination is a force to be reckoned with!

The next weeks were not easy. I missed the drugs terribly and could not believe I was acting like an addict. Denier, who still did not believe that anything had ever happened to me, was out in full force. As far as he was concerned, my reality was all in the present and I'd experienced no childhood abuse. I told Yael that she should try to speak with him during our session, but I had little hope he would change his mind. It was extremely important for me to have a part who didn't believe what had happened in my childhood, especially after the misery and tumult of getting drug-free. Since Denier had been out for years, it was not always easy to figure out why he was present at certain times and completely absent at others, but I needed him so I could continue to function.

EMAIL TO YAEL

Someday there will be a machine. You will sit next to it and plug your brain in. It will spit out a computer printout of all your memories, highlighting the difficult ones with magic ink so that you need not read them until you are ready. Whenever that is, you will take them to a therapist trained in EMDR where you will process those memories rapidly since you will not have to struggle to either remember them or believe them. This machine never lies, never embellishes, and never judges, except to warn you of what may be painful to learn. Many reasonable people might say that until this machine is up and running, they will take a pass in therapy. I wish I could explain more eloquently how it feels to slowly lose the integrity of your mind, and how difficult and unsettling it is to try to regain it. I no longer really know if the memories are more painful than the task of reconnecting the pathways that are my mind. Every session brings a new challenge, and every day I am more exhausted than the day before. There is no road map, no familiar path, no sense of what the other side feels like. For those who love to travel without knowing where they are going, or what language they will need to speak, this would be an adventure. Unfortunately, I prefer to have a plan, structure, the ability to communicate, a sense of where I will end up, what the weather will be like, and the hope that I will be happy at the end of the journey.

Whenever I go to a dark place, I think this must be the worst it will get. I cannot fathom greater pain when I am in the middle of despair, although I can imagine that it will not end. I don't even know why this all feels so much harder, scarier, more threatening than a few months ago. Instead of the goal appearing within reach, it feels like it is being sadistically pulled farther and farther away from me. I have not felt whole of late though one might say that I never really was. Wherever I might have been, it felt shattered. And those pieces of glass—they are sharp, they draw blood, they are near impossible to put together. And if reassembled, there are still a million cracks which make the whole both fragile and imperfect.

It is 7 weeks since I stopped drugs. I still miss them every day, many times a day. I wonder often why I am so resistant to taking medications, even with all of the rationale that I have expressed. I think that there is that piece of me—we met him/her this week—who feels so loathsome, so completely deserving of the abuse, that the thought of sedating me without exorcising this part is horrifying. This toxic core is them—it cannot be medicated away, nor will it go without a fight. I am afraid of hurting you—it is always on my mind and it makes for a lot of noise in the room.

I did not think I needed much space this weekend, but I was clearly wrong. So many times, I believe that I can trick my mind into forgetting, but it is the reverse and my mind is doing the tricking. In the end, I am so lost and confused, so eager for the cloud to lift and so unable to make it happen.

I am sorry to infuse this into your life right now, but it is what it is, I guess. I know that you have a greater than normal capacity to carry pain, but I still regret having to add on mine.

chapter 17

Dr. Steinberg

After the catharsis of the detox, Yael suggested I see a psychiatrist for a consultation. I resisted the idea because a psychiatrist would likely prescribe medication, which I opposed. But my continuous journeys into darkness overtook me, and I agreed, although parts of me remained incredibly resistant, and all of me wondered which alters would be medicated and would it be right for only some of them. I wanted to see a doctor who understood DID and ritual abuse, and at the same time, I did not want to have to tell my story again. Yael left a message for Dr. Marlene Steinberg, who had written *The Stranger in the Mirror*, a book in which she introduced the questionnaire that is used by many therapists to identify patients with DID. Dr. Steinberg was practicing in Northampton, Massachusetts, and I thought that two hundred miles would be the perfect distance separating me and my psychiatrist. The reality of sharing my parts with someone other than Yael was too much for the system to absorb.

Dr. Steinberg

Email to Yael

Writer is shut down.

There is a big battle going on with Butch/Romeo who has pretty much halted the process. They wrote in their journal but they won't write to you.

The littlest ones are OK with Steinberg—the older ones have been trying to have some input but there is little if any coherent thought happening here.

7 hopes she is nice.

Joey is worried she won't believe him and then you won't either.

Night says why bother?

Ciao.

Email from Yael

Not surprising that there are many feelings about the call to Marlene. Please reassure everyone that this is only a consult, and our work is a collaborative process, with consideration for all of your parts' varied needs. I think it can only be helpful, not harmful. It is impossible to sway my belief about what happened to you.

Although I had agreed to have a consultation, I still struggled with the decision to take or not take medication. I found it to be a common conflict among my baby-boomer peers who suffered from depression and were resistant to taking anything for it. We were children of the 1960s, used to illegal drugs but unwilling to take any that were prescribed. It was one of our many inconsistencies.

Then, my feelings shifted and I journaled:

Dr. Steinberg

Feeling miserable. Woke up today with that familiar wave of nausea that feels like grief. Every awakening, every morning, it is the same feeling. A thunderbolt of loss—of my life, my sanity, my resilience, my spirit. Every day I have to do battle with the demons who are trying to obliterate my hope. And so today begins the same. Leaving the kids is harder + harder, especially as they cling to me as if I will never return. Now home again, + deciding to stay here rather than join them at a birthday party—you would think the decision was as weighty as going to war. I should go—it will help me to feel better. I should stay—it will aggravate me. I should go—it will be nice to see everyone. I should stay—I am too depressed + too depressing to be around anyone. I should stay—that is what Yael would say—I should have some time alone. And so I do. Lili weeps disappointedly, saying that she thought I was coming, that she is sad, that she will miss me. And so, they leave. And I cry. And I don't know what to do with myself. I want to be in motion, I do not want to be home alone, thinking about my life, or lack of one. It is time for meds. Too much time is passing me by. I will never survive this for a few more years. My family will not survive it. Of course, now I can't be on something quick enough—now that I have convinced Yael that I will never take anything—now I must wait until we find someone who understands DID + meds + me.

I am dying here. I don't even want to figure anything else out. I don't care if I ever have another memory or insight or epiphany. If I felt better, who cares?

I am angry, withdrawn, anxious, sullen, dark + miserable. I hate work, I hate free time, I hate no time, I hate my parents, I hate that Tim Russert died and I didn't. I hate that even Flan-

nery cannot cheer me up, + worse, I can't even really have a conversation with her. I don't know who I am, where I am, what I want. I am all jumbled up. I want to be numb. Drugged. High. Gone. I want to see colors again, feel turned on, get excited, laugh until I cry. I want to be someone else. Anyone else. Just not me. I am so sick of myself. So disgusted. So bored.

EMAIL TO YAEL

I don't know if this is short-lived, but I feel so ready to be on medication.

I have been waking up, not only all night long, but every morning, with a wave of nausea that I now associate with grief. It is a sickening feeling of seeing a reality that I do not want to see, of feeling all the loss in my life, both past and present, that I no longer can ignore, deny, or block out.

It has been hard to identify what I might need given the amount of noise in my head and the frequency with which panic or despair overwhelm any other feelings. I guess that I have been surviving, of late, and survival is not good enough. I cannot stand to be around myself much longer, and I'm not sure that my family or staff or friends can stand it much longer either.

But mostly, I cannot imagine continuing this way for another year, or two, or four. I have reached that point where I am completely resistant to discovery because I am afraid that I cannot handle it. This is either the wall that one hits in a marathon, and I can pass through it, or it is simply insurmountable as such.

I still hoped Dr. Steinberg would have some other clues about healing that did not require meds. What I always thought was profound ambivalence about everything turned out to be different parts of my psyche arguing. The more voices I heard, the crazier I became and the more schizophrenic I felt. I, of course, did not know what it felt like to be schizophrenic, but Yael repeatedly assured me that I wasn't. She did, nevertheless, believe that treating my depression with medication would make it easier and not harder to uncover memories and to enable my parts to communicate. I had many concerns.

EMAIL TO YAEL

Do you think that we could spend some time getting to know everyone a little better before I learn how to take care of them?

It feels like you are asking me to take care of children whom I barely know. It is like babysitting for the first time, and not knowing who the kid is, what they like, need, or want. It makes me anxious and I feel like a failure. And I'm not yet convinced that I want to take care of them. I struggle at times to understand Lili and Ruthie, to know their rhythms, when they need space and when they need to be held, what will set them off and what will soothe them. I know what colors they like, who is their favorite princess, how they like their clothes to feel, which songs will lull them to sleep. And I love them unconditionally.

I get that this is the goal here, to love all of my inner kids that same way, and I even get in some way that they are really part of me. But I don't really feel it yet. I have moments of recognition, and moments of genuine love and compassion. But often, I don't know who they are. I have not lived with them for long and I need to. I know that you are trying to invite them into the room, but in the absence of context, they do not know what to say. I do not know how to give them this context except to be more patient with them so that they can tell their own stories.

I'm not sure why I am feeling all of this now. It has been a difficult month or so in therapy, where I have been feeling out of sorts, inadequate, not understood, angry and frustrated. It feels like I am not reacting well to the process, and maybe this is why. Not sure. Maybe this is a place I have to pass through, and I don't like it.

I will think about it all some more. You can too. Trying to pry Night off of me so that I can go to this fucking concert tonight and have some fun.

Night was a dark alter who had no gender and felt like a blanket of despair. It often came out at night and was coupled with Raven and Hate. They leaned heavily upon me, suffocating me, and leaving me unable to see joy in anything.

EMAIL TO YAEL

Spoke to Steinberg. Seeing her Tues 7-15 at five (1½ hrs) and Wed 11 am (1½ hrs).

Big fight with Suze about her not going and my making the decision without her. I'm feeling just a bit smothered and angry.

She charges twice as much as you do so I will never complain again about your fee. Add a hotel, the cost of the car and gas, and lost income...

Been agitated all day and now I'm even worse.

A several-hour consultation with a big name in the field of DID was a huge deal, and Susie responded appropriately by wanting to go with me, but I decided to see Dr. Steinberg on my own. It was a three-hour trip to Massachusetts, and I was psyched about traveling there. I love driving and being alone in the car, blasting music. It had never occurred to me to have Susie join me, although in hindsight, that was a perfectly reasonable suggestion on her part. At the time, however, it was way too much of an admission of my own anxiety to ask for or allow support from her.

EMAIL FROM YAEL

I think you are anxious about the whole trip—throw Susie's feelings into the mix—no room, and not good.

I think going to see Marlene is a courageous decision and another move toward health.

Hang in there! Let me know if you want to have Susie come in this week.

Now that I was off my drugs and needing some relief, I started to drink. I cannot drink much without getting drunk and slurred, so I only drank when I went out, which wasn't often. Fortunately, although garbled, I was a sweet drunk.

EMAIL TO YAEL

drunk. Love you. "cloud" is awesome. memories are gruesome. life is up and down. not wanting to see steinberg. need to cry more. not responsible for anything I say here. friends are nice. life is short. my kids are beautiful. my wife is funny. my parents suck. sleeping pills rock. therapy is long. chocolate is perfect. exercising is boring. email is the magical high-speed connection of life.

Dr. Steinberg

sometimes too high speed.
another day…gone by.

When I finally met with Dr. Steinberg, she suggested that my parts could be helping me and should come out more. I questioned this, but found her quirky and masterful at distinguishing, gathering, organizing, and weaving together everything about me. I was relieved when she didn't prescribe medication. She gave me, instead, a little book called *If I Could Mend Your Heart* by Mary I. Farr, with inspirational messages and a guide to emotional health.

However, having a DID expert affirm my diagnosis freaked me out a little. Afterward, I wrote a long email to Yael saying I was shocked to discover that I *really* might be a multiple and surprised at how vulnerable and detached I became during our consultation.

Email to Yael

It has been a pretty big and emotional week. Of course, the high from the trip is gone, the reality of life is settling in, the enormity of the work yet to be done is hovering overhead, and I am so ready for you to come back [from vacation] and for your feet to hit the streets of New York.

I have had neither the time nor the energy to write down my many thoughts. This is not the best time to start—at 11:50 at night…nevertheless…

I do not believe that any conscious part of me felt that Steinberg would negate the diagnosis of DID. But as I sat there being interviewed, prodded, probed, and picked apart as she would any DID patient, I was kind of shocked. I was as familiar talking about de-

personalization and identity alteration as I would be talking about tennis. I was not puzzled by anything she asked—I had a sinking kind of feeling and one of coming home at the same time…

Although I left Northampton with all kinds of hopes and plans and renewed energy and enjoyed singing really loudly to my own songs in my own car, my elevated mood only lasted one day. By last night, I was my old cranky self, and I was swearing at Steinberg's earnest proposal to comfort my inner parts and to dialogue with them. She has moved past comfort as the key to happiness and health and has added dialogue. Ongoing, constant dialogue between all parts at all times—no one can be left out, excluded, forgotten.

The idea of this is quite genius. The execution, however, is mind-boggling. She might imagine that all these parts have discernible personalities such that they can be reckoned with on the spot. It is one thing to be quick on your feet when you have more than one kid at home. It is quite another to be breaking up fights between 6 or 8 or 12 parts. Steinberg feels that my ambivalence, and at times my paralysis, represents my internal struggle between parts. She heard a "lot of conflict" going on. I think she is right but reining in those who are dueling is pretty hard when I do not yet know who they are.

Other things she said, in short: my "doctor" has to do a much better job of taking care of everyone; Doc has been resistant to stepping into the mess of my brain. my "doctor" also needs a little more mothering—from me, of course.

I need to schedule time to comfort everyone, several times each day. I need to dialogue that often as well.

I need to expand the places where my parts come out, besides the shower. Widen the joy, expand the repertoire. we talked about the following parts and what they need…(I took notes)

Also, we talked about couples therapy, what to tell friends and others, abreacting and discovering parts, organizing my life, and why Carol missed the boat.

She [Dr. Steinberg] is one strange cookie. She is clearly not comfortable in her own skin. She must have been the tall gawky nerdy girl who appears asexual and not terribly warm. She laughs at odd times and is not quite humorless, but close. She is so firm in her directions that you dare not say you can't do something. And yet, she is quite compassionate. But not terribly empathetic. She is not interested in hearing too much about your pain—either because it serves no purpose, or it distracts you and her from the task at hand which is to get rid of symptoms. She is not dismissive, nor does she rush you through the pain to get practical, but she doesn't linger either. There is no sadness in her eyes when you feel sad. And yet, she is not cold. Her voice and her tone rarely changed, except for the rare sidestep into something personal, when she seemed awkward and not as self-assured. She did tell me that she googled me and read a lot of wonderful things that patients had written about me and the practice. This was sweet and weird and made me strangely uncomfortable, maybe because she told me this early on. She has little respect for most other therapists, especially analysts. You of course received high marks for your rapid diagnosis. She does not believe in resistance but feels that some parts do not know how else to act and so they can't change without modeling. She is spiritual and yet pragmatic and disciplined. She expects the same from her patients.

I give you all this, not only because it is interesting to me and maybe to you, but because of how she was able to affect me, and how surprised I was. That I dissociated, cried, and felt on the verge of complete hysteria, all the time not knowing her well nor feeling completely safe, was really puzzling to me. I almost felt as though I were played like a rare musical instrument by a person who knew the instrument but not the person who embodied it. I did not want to go to where I went, but there was something almost hypnotic happening and I did. And then, after three and a half hours, I was left spent, hungry, exhausted, and young. She did offer me a yogurt, but I declined. Still, I was determined to not appear more needy than I already had been.

And so. I am home and happy to be here. I have no clue how to find the time in my life for all the homework that she assigned. But you and I will figure that out together. She also thinks that I am still working too much and she was not terribly sympathetic when I protested.

She is not writing anything up formally (she said she would have to charge me for the time to generate a report which pissed me off given her fees). She would be happy, however, to speak with you and will call you or you can call her. I did sign a release, but it was vague as to who would call whom.

There may be more but there is nothing left in my brain right now.

Safe home. I am glad that you are back. And I am glad that you are you.

After my meeting with Dr. Steinberg, the therapeutic process was a slow one, but I saw glimmers of clarity. In my work with Yael, I acknowledged that I was subtler than some multiples, who spoke different languages and wore different clothes for different parts. However, Susie and others told me that my voice and face shifted markedly in different settings and situations. All I could be certain of was that my internal voices were gradually becoming more recognizable to *me*. This realization was the beginning of my regaining some control over myself.

Still, the sessions with Yael continued to be devastating at times and bled into my outer life. Patients were concerned and I dodged their questions. I was rough with Lili during her meltdowns and I had tremendous shame about this, so Susie and I decided to tell the girls—who were about seven years old at this point—that I was dissociative. Susie handled it beautifully. She explained why I appeared angry or seemed inattentive and forgot things they told me. She assured them I was getting better and that my moods had nothing whatsoever to do with them. They listened, asked a few questions, and went back to their games.

Telling the kids' therapists was truly frightening, as I felt responsible for so much of their pain. I was embarrassed and humiliated and sometimes too panicked to speak, and so Susie would update them on my life as a multiple. More often than not, however, I still participated in our parent consultations and was present…for most of them. At one time, we had ten therapists, including psychiatrists, for our family of five.

Years later, some of my friends could even joke about which part they were talking to or which part did something that was questionable. At the same time, no one except Susie knew how difficult it was for me to go through the process of recovery, and no one brought casseroles the way they do when someone is sick or there's been a death in the family.

chapter 18

Abreactions, Memories, and Eighteen Parts

By the end of my first year working with Yael, I had uncovered eighteen alters and the process of discovery was overwhelming. I had unearthed little ones, big kids, teenagers, and grown-ups, and new ones were still appearing. Fortunately, Yael was able to keep track of everyone and had established special relationships with each part. I struggled to make sense of it all and was desperate for the process of discovery to be over.

EMAIL TO YAEL

There is a large, 1,000-small-piece, unfinished jigsaw puzzle in the middle of the dining room table which is in the middle of the family living space. A family of eighteen lives in the house. They have not eaten at the dining room table since the puzzle was begun more than one year ago. No one knows what the puzzle will finally look like although the writer in the family has imagined the finished product.

Abreactions, Memories, and Eighteen Parts

Everyone has worked on it, though the little ones have taken pieces and hidden them, and the teenagers have tried to resist the temptation to become involved, complaining that the puzzle is boring and doesn't do anything. They are disdainful of the family's joy and enthusiasm to finish and at the same time, secretly wish they could openly enjoy the process. Everyone feels conflicted when a missing piece is found, happy to see the picture forming, but jealous that they were not the ones to find it. At night, the puzzle lays still. It has no life without the family and no color. No one knows when it will ever get finished. Sometimes, when it is quiet, the mother goes to the puzzle and works on it. She recognizes where each piece came from and knows which child placed it. She also finds the hidden pieces and puts them back on the table. She silently wishes that the puzzle-making would be finished and that the family could perhaps all eat together again. She feels lonely for she is truly alone.

Many people knew what I was like before a session and after a session, but no one was ever quite sure what went on during my time with Yael. Many times, I wasn't so sure myself. Once I had met some of the gang and knew that they had a lot of stories to tell, I realized that dissociating was not only permissible in therapy but desirable. It gave me answers. It informed Yael. It moved us along.

Abreacting was a different story. Abreaction means to relive a traumatic experience in order to purge or resolve the emotional content of the memory. During the first years of therapy, I had few memories that were not abreacted at the same time. My dissociated selves carried the information but were incapable of recalling or speaking it. Furthermore, some of my parts were fragments, meaning they carried some memories, but they were not fully formed alters and had no context for the memory except the memory itself.

One memory, which was abreacted, found me inside a green metal box while an electrical current was used to torture me. I was unable to tell Yael what I was remembering, but I relived it and in so doing, acted out the abuse and the pain. I crouched in the corner of her office and behaved like a current was going through my body. I shook for minutes until Yael could calm me down and the abreaction stopped. She was able to guess what was happening and I could tell her later that she was right and fill in some details.

Sometimes it felt like I was on autopilot—I arrived at Yael's office ready to explode, and within minutes I was abreacting the worst of my ritual abuse memories. These were the hardest to relate because they were so extreme and so difficult to believe. I will never know whether some of the sacrifices I saw in a memory were staged by my abusers or actually happened, but I do know that it was one or the other, and that as a baby and toddler, everything was real and terrifying to me.

There was no question that reliving these memories was traumatic, and Yael constantly questioned whether this re-traumatization was necessary, but whenever we tried to skirt the abreactions, the gang protested, and the system went out of whack. The abreaction dissipated the panic and de-weaponized the memory. A functioning system had me going to work and living my life with some degree of normalcy and a quiet brain. An out-of-whack system had me dissociated, panicked, and listening to *all* my parts yammering at the same time. There were days when Yael and I both questioned the process and kept hoping that there was an easier way.

Abreactions, Memories, and Eighteen Parts

Sometimes an active and dramatic session was followed by an exhausted peacefulness. This could occur after abreactions as well, and I likened it to electroshock therapy—or what I imagined that to be. It felt as if all my brain cells were shocked into submission, and I would then feel less depressed for a night or a day or even a few days. Then, the buildup would begin anew, with different memories screaming to be heard. I wondered if Yael had these same cycles. I know that there were times when I felt a whole lot better than she did—as if I had passed my pain to her. There were also times when my abreactions left me disconnected and spacey but left her horrified.

Sometimes Yael asked for an alter to come into the room. Often, they arrived spontaneously, or they came out while I was coloring, which my little ones loved to do. It was always startling to both of us when a new part appeared, for they were so self-contained and so distinctly different from one another.

My therapy and memories affected me at work, and I had panic attacks and many moments of deep despair. Yael and Dr. Steinberg suggested I take six months off, but I refused. Seeing patients who had survived their own abuse made me even more empathetic than I had previously been.

As a physician, I needed to focus on what I was doing and because I loved being a doctor, that wasn't hard for me to do. Doc had what so many of my other alters did not—self-awareness and self-esteem. If I said that the process of uncovering my memories did not impact me at work, I'd be lying. There were many days when I did not think I could make it through office hours because I was having panic attacks or because I was in such despair over what I was remembering. But Doc had an uncanny ability to function and to function well, despite the emotions that might accompany her to work.

Abreactions, Memories, and Eighteen Parts

Doc, however, did *not* want to take care of the gang. At all. And for good reason. It took a lot of discipline and pure grit to shut out the noise. Doc's work, which included running the practice with her partners, was not easy, although it was clearly easier than being a mom and the pay grade was pointedly better.

I wrote in my journal:

So Doc has been busy. Now she has 4 fantastic partners, 4 other doctors, 2 midwives, 1 physician assistant, 3 nurse prac-titioners, 1 administrator, 4 nurses and a staff of 50. Three of my partners, Audrey, Dorothy, and Suzanne, and one previous partner, Leslie, my CFO Debbie, and one of my nurses, Susan, were all with me when my personality shattered into pieces 11 years ago.

It would have helped both my parts and my family if they were able to have their needs met by Doc, but that did not happen. Even later in therapy, when I understood that all my alters needed my attention and that Yael would not be there forever to do the caretaking, Doc never really stepped in. At least not consciously. In all fairness, Doc was working at keeping the gang quiet so she could work. And not surprisingly, the gang would grow noisier before it quieted down.

chapter 19

Tommy and Separation Anxiety

Tommy was a complicated and likable teenage boy. He was fourteen, lean and strong. He wore jeans falling off his hips, a white T-shirt with a cigarette pack in his sleeve, and sneakers. His hair was light brown, thick and longish. He saw himself as a cowboy of sorts; he loved horses and dogs and riding fast in the car. He was a risk-taker for sure, often cocky but also sullen at times. He hated that we were not more athletic as we had been during my teenage years and argued vehemently for more exercise. His sense of responsibility was unmatched, and he took care of the little ones in the gang without fail.

He carried the weight of the world on his young shoulders. One of his struggles that would continue throughout our work was that Tommy was trapped in my body—now that of a fifty-eight-year-old woman—and he was not at all happy about it. In fact, he was downright pissed. Although I never wore girly-girl clothes, except from the ages of one to four, I still could not dress like a fourteen-year-old boy. I tried and some days I did better by him than others.

Susie and I were busy raising Lili and Ruthie, which consumed most of our time when we were not working. Tommy cut a deal with Yael: if she would stop picking her cuticles and nails, Tommy would start exercising or find a sport. Within months, Yael's nails were beautiful, and Tommy had not done a thing, expecting that he would have a lot longer to work out his end of the deal. That took another six years.

Tommy cared for all the little ones but was dissociated from his own pain—pain that he did not believe existed. He felt life began at fourteen and he did not accept that we all shared one body and one horrific history. Tommy could not get the hang of therapy. He struggled with Yael because he did not know how to talk to a woman and because he could not and would not cry. He was difficult at home with Susie and wouldn't listen to any feedback from her about his behavior, which could be cruel when he teamed up with Raven and **Fuckface**. Together, they wreaked havoc, from driving recklessly to making rude comments to strangers.

———————

Therapy did not change all that much over the next many months. My sessions were dramatic and intense, and it was hard to see that I was in fact getting well. Slowly but surely there were more glimmers of light penetrating my days, and more importantly, I was getting used to having so many people living inside of me. What began as noise in the cafeteria became discernible voices in my head, and they made it clear to me that they would no longer be ignored.

Separating from Yael went from excruciating to tolerable and eventually to fine. But that would take years, and my first big separation came in the spring of 2009. She was going to Israel for two weeks and the anticipation for me was overwhelmingly dreadful. I was still fragile while having wild mood swings and felt forever dependent upon her. My internal little ones were particularly frightened by the thought of having only me to take care of them. I was still so busy trying to survive that I was not all that good at checking in with all my parts to see what their needs were. Cutting that umbilical cord with Yael, albeit temporarily, seemed impossible. Yael had given this a lot of thought and wrote me cards ahead of time which I opened while she was gone. This calmed me sufficiently so that I could mobilize enough strength to let her go emotionally. But Susie and the kids got so sick the day before she left that I could not leave the apartment for my last appointment.

EMAIL TO YAEL

So here is my bon voyage for you. I would much have preferred to deliver it in person, but that was not in the stars, or the moon (full as it has been) for today.

I also hoped that I would have had more time to check in with the gang to see how they were all feeling, but that was not meant to be, either.

Finally, I would have liked that this missive be delivered after a good night's sleep and some uncluttered reflection, but...

Often, these departures/separations are like dreams—it is about what you make of them. In the end, these past few days have forced some reshuffling inside—a kind of post-electro-shock calm, a reordering of priorities, a kind of replanting myself on the ground.

Tommy and Separation Anxiety

The anticipation of your departure has been the worst, especially, I think, for Tommy and the boys. They are still not used to owning their vulnerability and are definitely not familiar with unconditional love, such as yours. Tommy also feels that it is a little too soon to separate, given the confusing feelings for you that came up last week. He is certain that with time and distance, you will push him aside. Little Girl seems secure lately—she seems to get the unconditional love thing but is wondering where she will get her love and hugs from if she gets panicked. She is the most overtly excited about reading your notes. **Seven** *[another alter], of course, has been planning the memorial service for when your plane goes down, but she has not come to terms with the fact that if anything does happen to you, she cannot save you. She still expects earthquakes in her life and does not feel safe with you away. She has promised to lay low and to let the others live life until you get back. She will not only be excited to read your notes but will probably sleep with them and carry them around. Malcolm and Joey are mostly worried about Lili's outbursts and their reaction to her. So is Tommy. But they kept a copy of your email the other day where you assured them that they will not be violent and they promised to read your words when they get angry.* **Aimee** *[a smaller part who used to wait for Little Girl's abuse] will be waiting—that is what she does—but this time, she will be waiting for something happy. Ironically, she KNOWS that you will come back, but she will be surprised to see a different ending than she is used to. Night has not been around lately and we would prefer that it stay that way. We will be careful about what we watch and read while you are away so that that darkness is not triggered. But if it is, Night is not allowed to make any decisions* *until you return. Butch/Romeo—they cannot stand not seeing you, even if they are used to watching from afar. They love you and will always think that you are hot. And they don't really accept that they cannot have you.*

Writer is here and will probably come and go. All writing/emails etc. will be sent after you return, or we will read them together when we see you.

Doc will be fine, as will **Mom** *[an alter who kept an eye on me in the present], I suppose.* **Speedy** *[a rapidly moving and functional part] will probably take over at times and Denier will likely be out a lot. Of course, Flannery may make that difficult, since she is fiery and passionate and now well read, and she seems beyond certain that I was ritually abused. Denier will not miss you at all, but then we will not miss Denier someday.*

And then there is me. I should borrow a pet name that Ruthie and Lili would choose—like Heart Blossom or Rose or Grace or Heart Flower. I guess that when the others are quiet, or all in harmony, there is my own soul that remains. Often, I feel like a giant heart, wounded but beating, forcing life over death, but never taking anything for granted. I love you in a way that I have never loved before and never expect to again. You have absorbed my pain, found my spirit, warmed my soul, and in a moment of extreme generosity, you will let me go.

chapter 20

Baby, Little Shelley, More Tommy, Seven, Other Seven

I survived Yael's trip and soon we got back to work. I was becoming increasingly agitated and angry between sessions and having a harder time dealing with Lili, whose tantrums were escalating. I was afraid I would hurt her if she persisted in biting and kicking and punching me. And my apprehension was justified. I had all the normal anger that a parent can have, plus a truckload of rage left over from my abuse. Soon there was little distinction between the two, and I was terrified of what I might do to her. In an exchange of text messages with Yael, we wrote:

SK: *No good.*
Yael: *What do u mean?*
SK: *Can't explain I am not right Extremely agitated Cannot settle Angry and belligerent things feel distorted Brain not ok Waiting for Susie Home alone with Lili*

Yael: *What's Lili doing? When is Susie expected back?*

SK: *Lili playing near me Suze on way Can you stay close by? There is an earthquake in my head*

Yael: *Yes, I'm right here. Let me know when Susie gets back*

SK: *Suze home*

Yael: *Any better?*

SK: *Not really Feel like I should be on psych ward My eyes are funny I will try to write later if I can or might take a walk restless*

Yael: *Stay safe xoxoxoxoxo*

SK: *That is the challenge I suppose*

Unfortunately, this is how I was living. Sometimes I could write and feel a little better. Often nothing worked except the passage of time or making it to a session where I could explode safely. It turns out that I was indeed exploding at home as well although I didn't know it until later. I was physically rough with Lili when she was having her own meltdowns, and I could be terrifyingly angry. Most of the time, Susie was there to stop me, but the damage had been done. Built on a foundation stemming from my own abuse, my shame grew greater and greater.

I was writing either emails or text messages to Yael almost every day. Occasionally I had something good to say, but most of the time I was panicked, distraught, despairing, confused, hopeless, and enormously frustrated by the process of healing. I was constantly struck by the unfairness of being abused and how the path to health was so overwhelmingly stressful.

———————

Baby was a new part who emerged around this time, with visual and body memories limited to Jack Watkins and my mother. Baby was the first part to see them together in ways that in retrospect were inappropriate. Jack was around a lot when my father wasn't, and he had far too much access to my body, including inappropriate touching while changing my diaper. My mother followed his lead, as he told her that he knew what little girls needed because he already had two of his own. This was but a glimmer of the awful recollections that would arise over the coming years.

Another new young part to arrive was **Little Shelley**, who was pre-abuse and preverbal. She was curious, filled with wonder, and protected. She loved existing in the warmth of Yael's presence. Sadly, her innocence did not last long, and she had few memories of anything; she did recall that her mother held her at some distance.

EMAIL TO YAEL

You asked me about my essence, and I gave you Little Shelley. Me before and/or oblivious to the pain of my abuse. This is one of those times when I wish I understood how my brain works, how it searches for information, and then how it releases it. I was dumbfounded with what came out today, and with how easily information pours out once someone is tapped. I have no master plan that I can access, and I never would have imagined that Little Shelley had stayed so disconnected from what was happening. But, of course, it makes sense that she would remain while others were fracturing off. The few times I have been coloring and tapped one of the little ones, I have been mystified by the ease with which they remember and tell their stories. it is so effortless; it really leaves grown-up me feeling lost at the starting gate but watching in awe. of course it is so much easier to be taken care of, and without all that terror, I can absorb all your love and store it up for use later on. I wish the older ones did not have to fight so hard to let you in, but I guess that is their nature.

Little Shelley seems to carry my trust, my optimism, my need to see the glass half full. she loves to be loved and touched and talked to and she is happy to be in the moment. she sees the good in people, she has no speediness, no obsessions and no noise. she also knows more than she lets on, but she doesn't feel any pain. I don't know if she can cry—I'm not sure she has any need to, but if she did, it would probably be fine. she loves you and feels happy that she waited all these years to find you.

———

Little Shelley was one of the younger parts that Tommy took care of. Most multiples have a main alter or manager, one who knows all the players and is central to functioning in the past as well as the present. Tommy seemed always to be around, although when Yael and I first got to know him, he vehemently denied that he was present during the early years of abuse. He acknowledged that his job was to take care of all the little ones who had been hurt, but said he came along after the worst things had already happened. Despite being told that we all inhabited one body, Tommy was certain that he was not there early on.

About three years into therapy, Tommy began to open up, making room for other parts to do more work. One of Tommy's biggest allies was Seven (or 7), who was a suicidal seven-year-old girl who carried much of my depression. She was the first alter to appear without a specific memory of abuse. It would be many months before she uncovered what exactly had happened to her. But in the beginning, she arrived as an extremely sad little girl with her own alter.

She wrote:

...and no one really gets it, much as they all say they do, much as they try. This is 7. A dark cloud has descended, or perhaps night, and I am on a mission. It is a private one—the 1st time I am aware that I have another self. I am active, funny, competent + precocious. I am physically unstoppable + happiest when I am in motion, climbing a tree, riding a bike, playing ball. And I am depressed. 7 yr old depression—wow it is so sad + confusing but I know that I cannot talk about it. I don't really understand it, I know that I need someone to take care of me, someone to hold me long enough so that my pain goes away + the wall between my selves comes down. It is an aching that is way bigger than any 7 yr old should carry, an emptiness that drives me to feel desperate, and to feel that death may be the best option. 7 is when suicide entered my consciousness...

I was little then and old. I traveled in a grown-up world, only pretending childhood, but I knew that I didn't belong with other children. I knew that something in my life made me feel like childhood was gone, mine was gone.

Seven was depressed. **Other Seven** was happy. Together they survived the dramatic ups and downs of second grade, and fell in love with their teacher, who they thought might be the one to save them from desperate and sad loneliness. I blew my chances and, of course, never told her or anyone what I was feeling, or what I later learned had happened to me. In truth, I had already dissociated so even *I* didn't remember what had happened.

Baby, Little Shelley, More Tommy...

Seven took a long time to trust Yael. When she did, I started having new flashbacks. I remembered my family's move to Connecticut when I was four-and-a-half years old. I'd had screaming nightmares for the first year. My parents dutifully read Dr. Spock's *Baby and Child Care* and tried to comfort me, but I was inconsolable. I remember being terrified of the dark, the night, and being alone. Eventually, however, I must have begun to feel safe because I stopped having nightmares and life seemed normal. Of course, at this point, I had no memory of the abuse at all as I had dissociated throughout.

The next few years passed seamlessly, as much as I remember. I went to school and made friends and did whatever four-, five-, and six-year-olds do. The Watkinses stayed in touch with my parents but to the best of my knowledge, did not see us again until I was seven. According to my mother, Jack was insistent about visiting and wanted to "see the kids," meaning me and my brother. This was peculiar, but my mother, who remained enamored of Jack, didn't think much of it.

I started having flashbacks in therapy about that visit. I had already remembered that I was a depressed seven-year-old who fantasized often about death and was desperate for attention from my teacher. I wanted someone to know how sad I was, but had no idea how to communicate this, and had already been conditioned and programmed not to speak, so I tried in many nonverbal ways to get attention. I was aware at seven that I was split in half, and that I had a part who went to school and played with friends and a part who was extremely fragile and alone.

When the Watkinses came to visit, my parents left me alone with them to take my brother to a Little League game. Jack and his wife, Virginia, who also belonged to the cult, called me downstairs to the guest room in our house. I went, with no memory of who they really were, although I have since chastised myself repeatedly for going down those stairs.

Together, they tried to rape me, but god only knows why and how I struggled, kicked, screamed, and fought for my life. When Jack could not penetrate me vaginally, he turned me over to rape me anally. At this moment, I split off and called for Tommy to come help me. This became our memory.

Jack became furious and dragged me into a tiny bathroom next to the boiler, and away from Virginia. He took my hair and pulled my head back and forth, hitting it on the bathroom wall, and then he forced himself into my mouth. When he was done, I went upstairs and showered and scrubbed myself clean. Tommy was with me the whole time.

The only other thing I remembered is that when the Watkinses were leaving, they told my parents what a nice time they had had with me.

I stood there in silence. I was completely dissociated.

I later remembered that Jack had telephoned during the years before they came and promised me that they would see me again. I was always waiting, and I realized that they were keeping my programming intact.

That was the last I saw of them. Ever. They sent Christmas cards to my parents, who stayed in touch. Many years later, when I told my parents what had happened, they stopped their contact with them. There was never a confrontation or conversation or anything. Now, in retrospect, that was also terribly strange.

Dealing with Seven in therapy was heartbreaking. She remained sad and closed off for many months after having this memory. Whatever Yael did to take care of her was never enough. It never penetrated her despair. This was also one of the first times that we became aware of how much programming the cult had done; how they had used mind control to keep me in a dissociated state and to keep me silent. The programming also manifested in my reactions to certain dates, holidays, sounds, numbers, and visual stimuli like crosses, pentagrams, hooded figures, and masks.

I recounted my experience with the Watkinses many times, much to Yael's sorrow. I thought about Flannery, Lili, and Ruthie at seven—how little and vulnerable they were, and how unfathomable it was that I was raped at that age and did not talk about it to anyone. I wanted to find more details and absolve myself of responsibility for the whole awful experience. I was left with grief, guilt, and shame because I felt that I should have known not to be alone with the Watkinses while my parents were gone.

EMAIL TO YAEL

Bad night. kept waking up with too much going on in my brain. wondering why i keep going back over and over and over again. i think that i am trying to retrieve all of the feelings that got sequestered away but only the terror and the noise are here. i can't get to the sadness, the grief, the vulnerability because other stuff drowns it out and so I'm left feeling unfinished all the time. parts of me want to go back and do it over, do it right, tell what happened and be heard, get taken care of, move on. seven cannot believe that no one knew, that she did not tell, that she carried all that pain around and that still she cannot cry. everyone feels stuck in some whirlwind of visual and auditory madness but there is no relief except it is quieter when it ends. not done though. never done. i feel hardened beyond repair at times, too cold and walled off to really feel. but they are in there, the feelings, teasing me from within some locked box, with flash cards guarding the gate, and programming scrambling the directions to get there. this is what leaves me feeling hopeless. the pieces, so many pieces. i can't really keep track, and i never know where i might go on any given day, at any moment, like i am still under a spell somehow. see you later.

This was also Tommy's memory and it was the first time that he could acknowledge that he too was abused. His involvement in the rape occurred when Jack turned Seven over and said that he would rape her like he would a boy. But the rest of the memory was Seven's and Tommy only reappeared afterward in the shower to help her clean up. He did not carry the sense of responsibility that Seven did, for she felt that she should have known that something terrible was going to happen and should not have gone downstairs. Despite having dissociation explained to her many times, she could never absolve herself of responsibility, and so added to her grief were guilt and shame. For Seven, this has never fully gone away.

Because Tommy could recall fragments of Seven's trauma, he finally realized he was a multiple himself. He had repressed all his earlier memories and believed initially that his life started at fourteen. The more we worked with Yael, the harder it became for Tommy to hold it together. He began to have his own flashbacks and memories but did not want to abreact and lose control. We found that doing EMDR by tapping him helped him to process the trauma. Unlike my own initial reaction to EMDR, it worked for Tommy, in part because he liked the quietness of EMDR and apparently the buzzers did not bother him. Later, he benefitted from hypnosis.

Baby, Little Shelley, More Tommy . . .

However, he struggled and remained fragile for a long time. He wanted to go back to the way things were before he remembered anything.

hi it's tommy, it is three am and i can't sleep. i don't know why it is so hard to talk but it feels like my bein a guy and talking cannot exist on the same planet. the problem is that i am not only a boy and so i feel like talkin but nothing comes out. i don't know what a broken heart feels like but i think i have one. i think i'm really unhappy cause i feel trapped and confused and lonely. i was doin ok taking care of everyone and i thought i was really strong and could handle anything but then i started to feel bad and feel the same way the others felt and started to feel panic and agitated and like memories were coming up and it is an awful feeling and i didn't feel so much stronger or better than anyone else. maybe worse cause i didn't have me to take care of me. i'm not sure about letting you do it cause you're a girl and there's all this power stuff and sex and feelings mixed in and you know about alice so you get the whole trust thing. and when i grew up i helped make butch/ romeo and lived inside a girl but still got to be in charge and didn't have to remember anything or really talk about feelings and i just had sex all the time which felt a whole lot better than this does. only truth is i was starting to unravel a bit then too and at night i would write all this painful stuff and didn't understand where it was all coming from but it would pour out and i would wake up the next day and be back to my old self. i sometimes didn't even know what i wrote but i guess it made me feel better somehow. i still wanted to kill myself at night when i wrote but not so much during the day which was the opposite of seven who wanted to kill herself during the day mostly. seven mostly wanted to get killed saving someone's life cause she felt so ashamed and worthless but i don't really care so much about that and i just want to go out with a bang like a crash or a jump or blowing my brains out and sometimes i even think about taking a few people with me just for fun. you see i'm really not all that nice except when i'm around the little ones cause i love them a lot and they didn't get much chance to have any fun like i did. so Hate comes at night and he is my buddy and he doesn't talk at all but he writes some always with his left hand. anyway i was saying that i'm really confused now and kind of cracking a bit and i'm not really sure even who I am anymore. there is all this noise in my head and fear and no one to trust for sure and my body hurts so much but if you touch it it doesn't always feel safe and i want it to but I have to be careful you know. that's why Butch/Romeo disappeared a long time ago cause they figured that they might ruin everything for the whole gang if they tried to have sex with you and if you rejected them...well no one ever did that before so who knows what they would do but it would be painful for sure. i know you think that maybe my cracking is a good thing, cause therapists always like it when walls come down but i'm not liking it much at all and the timing sucks too. by the way when i was put into the water and I was so freaked out I was really young which is why i let you take care of me but that doesn't mean anything really and i was so busy drowning that i couldn't think about much else especially sex so it was cool. see you.

When it came to Tommy, being in a relationship with Susie proved to be complicated. Not only did Susie have to deal with Raven and his nastiness, but she had to spend a lot of her time with Tommy who was seriously an adolescent boy. He simply did not want to be a grown-up with big responsibilities and a family, outside of his own internal one, to take care of. He often could not handle any feedback from Susie that was negative, especially about things like his driving, his know-it-all mentality, and his belief that he was indestructible. He also could not talk about his feelings, which added to an already stressful marriage. Tommy was cozy with Raven and Fuckface, and they were all emotionally abusive and terribly unpleasant to be around.

After two years of abreacting memories, and after many months of Yael pleading for a different way of working together, we started to interrupt my abreactions. I had gotten into a familiar although never comfortable pattern of dissociating in sessions and going back to the darkest places. I felt like I needed to remember everything, down to the tiniest detail. Remembering, however, was agonizing and part of me (or some of us) realized that we could and should start to move on from the past. Yael also hoped that I could see the past and recount it without necessarily reliving it. She felt strongly that I need not abreact the same memory repeatedly. That was easier said than done. For one thing, I had older parts who had not yet remembered their abuse from when they were younger. Tommy—the central organizer and caretaker of the gang—continued to be dissociated himself and had more memories that were buried by his own alters. As painful as it was, I had become dependent on our way of working together, because it was a known, because I trusted that Yael would take care of me after each abreaction, and because I assumed that it was working okay.

Baby, Little Shelley, More Tommy . . .

The little ones are pretty much done remembering. Their little minds feel quieted. Not only do they not have much more to remember but even if they did, they do not really want to go there. They do, however, still want you to take care of them from time to time, play with them, check in with them, hold them...

Seven has not weighed in on any of this, FYI.

Tommy has more to remember but he is also not sure he needs to or wants to go back. He feels inadequate right now, and easily criticized. He feels that when you question whether we need to go back and to be back in a memory, that he is supposed to know what is right, but he doesn't. That was him who started to cry (albeit a little) earlier in the week because he was so exasperated by your questions and his inability to answer them. He also clearly wants to be taken care of and also cannot accomplish this without being in pain. It seems that pain for all of us has to be dramatic and devastating to even count, and that abreacting is the only way we recognize how much pain we have. That said, it became clear this week that you are able to interrupt an abre-action and that some of the time I seem to feel ok. At other times, I feel angry and frustrated. But I think—and this is where it gets tricky— that this is good for us. We have had little conflict and sadly, I think it's time that we had some. This pains me, seriously, but I guess like all good writers, I believe that there must be conflict for the story to move forward. And I think I am stuck in a pattern with you right now that feels comfortable, but maybe not provocative enough for growth.

There will, of course, be times when I am truly searching for something and need to go back and I haven't the foggiest idea how we will know which times those are, but you will ask and I will try to know. And Tommy will try to really think about it since he is the major organizer of the gang and our memories. And he may spar with you some, but I am hoping that sparring is good for the gang. I still need to dissociate to access all my parts, but maybe they can ask you for what they need in terms of care and nurturing without abreacting. Or not…guess we will see…

I don't expect this transition to be easy for me, even if I am initiating it. It requires a leap of faith, and the assumption that life is better on the other side of the canyon. Unlike giving up drugs, however, I do not expect to do a cold turkey on my abreacting. I do want you to keep challenging me, keeping me present, making me look at you, and questioning my reasons for reliving old pain. And I do expect that I will keep pushing sometimes to go back for reasons that I hope will become clear over time.

Tommy put it in his own words:

Email to Yael

i wasn't sure i was gonna come out again today cause i feel really fucked up in the head and i kind of want to go back to the way things were but that is not really happening. everyone is trying to please you or get your attention or your love and it is pissing me off big time. first of all, it occupies a lot of time in our brain which could be better spent having fun. and if we were having more fun then we wouldn't need to see you so much which could be good too. secondly, why put all this energy into a relationship that you know is gonna end. and thirdly, all of this talking is really hard for me, and even harder is having to feel stuff and to feel it in front of someone. i can't really get past the feeling that i'm gonna die talking or worse, crying. lately i thought i was gonna cry and even started to a few weeks ago but was able to stop before i looked like some blathering idiot. what would i do if i lost it with you? i don't think i could let you take care of me really and then I would be drenched in all this pain and you would say that's ok but then i think i would lose myself and then what? i already feel like i have lost a lot of myself and I'm not sure where all my helpers have gone. i know that there are others living inside me but before i could really know them they disappeared. i don't like needing help from anyone but i was used to all of my inside help so that didn't really count. now i can't even find my part who was taking care of the little ones cause I am so pissed at them for outing me in the first place. there was no reason you had to know that i was a multiple also but now that you do it means that you are gonna wanna know how all the pieces fit together which means more talking or more remembering or more something. and you are gonna wanna know who my helpers were and what i saw and that means more talking and more seeing me without my walls which again is so terrifying it makes it hard for me to breathe even. raven thinks i am really crazy to even write to you and denier says that you are trying to seduce me cause why else would you really care. this is all so confusing to me and i feel really stuck cause i can't walk away and i can't go forward and so i am stuck in hell here wondering if and when i will find my way out. without a map. and no way can i ask for directions. all this makes me want to die. Raven understands that.

---

can't write anymore. wish you just knew my mind. wish i could beam things to you. wish you weren't so soft and funny. i wish you could wrestle and try to hurt me so i could get angry and sweaty and mean and maybe things would shatter in me some more but maybe things would seem clearer and i wouldn't feel so sad and lost.

Like every other time in our work together, and after *much* discussion, Yael and I collaborated as we moved in a slightly new direction. We limited the amount of time I spent reliving a past memory, and at the same time allowed for new memories to come out when there was an urgency to do so. She asked me if I could draw a diagram of my parts, and I did.

That night I wrote:

Whoa. What a ride. Diagrammed the family today, leaving out some adult parts + perhaps several others. But as I wrote down each name or part, I felt their relief in being acknowledged, and at the same time, the spinning in my head was wild. The room was both quiet + filled with echoes of children's voices. My own head was fragmented + yet completely intact. And then, as everyone started to pipe in, the competition for attention became fierce. I could feel the pulling at each other, much as Lili + Ruthie do—"My turn, no it's my turn, no mine..." Yael kept better track of who was out than I did + it was all pretty wild. Of course I could not speak for a few hrs after, but as of now, I am left with a headache, psychic exhaustion + some peace. Certainly for the moment, the sadness of the past week is gone. I would love some time to think about what happened. Maybe later.

chapter 21

What Did Happen?

—————

With Yael, the recollections of ritual abuse came as flashes early on, but later emerged as complete memories—like how, when I was a baby, my mother allowed Jack to diaper me and carry me around. He had full access to me and plenty of alone time because he "watched" me while my mother ran out to do errands or pick up my brother at school. His fingers were all over me and inside of any opening he could find. I was anally and orally penetrated, but never vaginally as far as I remember. I realized much later in therapy that he was merely preparing me for much more horrible abuse. On my first birthday, he told me that he had something special for me. One of my older parts remembered later in therapy that he took me down to his cellar where he put his finger up my ass and he came in my mouth. I was choking and terrified and hated my birthday from that day forward.

I was too young to understand his threats, which came later as I got older, but I was cognizant enough to know that I was frightened and in pain and used to cry whenever he was present. He pulled my hair each time until I was trained to stop crying. He also showed my mother how to soothe me by stimulating me gently. Even as a small child, I was learning about arousal. This was the first of many crazy-making things Jack Watkins did to me that kept me confused and obedient. Eventually I stopped crying altogether and didn't really permit myself to cry again until I had worked with Yael for several years.

Ritual abuse was not a hot topic back in the 1980s when I had my first memories. I had already been in practice for ten years when they began. Everything I recalled seemed incredible from the start, and a great deal of my healing meant coming to terms with memories that even I did not believe. Today we live with acts of violence every minute of every day. We are also more educated about and open to the reality of sexual abuse and perversion. In fact, as lucidly described in *Safe Passage to Healing* by Chrystine Oksana, "Everything found in ritual abuse collectively (physical abuse, emotional abuse, sexual abuse, incest, sadistic violence, murder, drugs, deception, manipulation, conditioning based on punishment, and unbridled veneration of power) is known to occur independently in our society." She adds: "Ritual abuse combines all of the above. It is organized abuse carried out by a group to achieve power. The abuse aims to break a victim's spirit and to gain the ultimate in power—absolute control over another human being."[3]

To the best of my knowledge, I experienced no group or ritual abuse in my early months of life. The ritual abuse began sometime later, although

---

3 Chrystine Oksana, *Safe Passage to Healing: A Guide for Survivors of Ritual Abuse* (New York: HarperPerennial, 1994).

What Did Happen?

I was still essentially preverbal, and it lasted until I was four years old, at which time the Watkins family moved away from Fresh Meadows and so did we.

These memories came to me in one seemingly endless flood that lasted years. A flashback might arrive visually or as a body memory, with eventually all senses remembering each event. There was always an extreme perverted sexual energy in the room. The louder the chanting, the more aroused everyone became, and with that, sexual abuse or sadistic pleasure ensued, including animal and human sacrifice. I could smell, hear, see, taste, and touch every memory as it engulfed me, and still I was nowhere near feeling the grief, the tremendous sadness that I later came to feel.

It turns out that you cannot remember trauma once and then be done with it. There are a host of other emotions that come later in the process and are paralyzing in and of themselves. And as a multiple, or dissociated person, each memory is carried by one part, or sometimes two, and the different parts do not learn how to communicate with each other for a long time. So, I might have a complete memory, with all senses alerted, but not remember it the next day. Yael had to open those doors of communication repeatedly. She had to carry the story so that eventually I could own it. She had to keep track of each part—which eventually numbered thirty-one—by changes in my voice, my face, and my body language, and she had to communicate with each of them appropriately for their age and their temperament. Every part had a distinct relationship with her, and she with them.

Memories came in fragments, seemingly in some order divined by I don't know who or what. The more painful ones came later in the process; the ones involving my mother came last.

What Did Happen?

I remembered chanting and robes early on and knew that I was in the center of a circle. The noise was deafening, frantic, and frenetic. I was aware that bad things were about to happen, but the full picture did not emerge for weeks. By the time I remembered, I was already terrorized and at the same time, driven to see the final picture. I remained curious for several years, after which I thought that I had seen enough. That, however, did not stop new memories from coming or new parts from showing up. My wishes had little to do with the pace or the content of the process. Therapy became one giant exorcism.

EMAIL TO YAEL

Today was awful. I don't know for sure but this might have been my first ritual, and the first major split. The physical pain coupled with the arousal was excruciating. The scene was picture-perfect—no hazy fuzzy not sure this really happened type flashback. Jack's use of my mother's explicit consent crystallized the feeling of abandonment, heightened the terror and broke my little heart. I felt every molecule of your love today—it was as searing as the pain and I think I might have died right there without it. I hate seeing my pain in your eyes but I have come to understand how important it is—that bearing witness without feeling is simply not enough.

I was also conditioned and programmed to accept everything that happened to me and to feel certain ways at certain times. I did not understand the programming for some time, but every now and then I went to a dark and disturbing place, triggered by something I could not identify. What I did know was that certain dates drove me to the limit and did so annually:

Halloween, Christmas, Easter, and other holidays established in the satanic calendar. It always seemed like I was making progress and then suddenly I turned dark or suicidal or terrorized.

A cult will use programming to manipulate and initiate dissociation in its victims in order to freely abuse them without objection. According to Oksana, "To achieve this, violators make use of human learning and developmental patterns. For example, it is known that most lifelong beliefs and resulting behaviors have their roots in the crucial early developmental years. It is also believed that dissociative learning happens more readily at this time. Therefore, cult indoctrination is likely concentrated before the age of six. Dissociative training may start at birth."

I was programmed to be still, not make a sound, not cry, and know when terrifying things were about to happen. I was threatened to not tell a soul about what I experienced and if I did, my abusers would kill me or my family. I came to believe everything they said and knew that all of it must be kept secret. I was told that what happened was my responsibility and so I also felt guilt and shame that lasted well into my adulthood when I finally got help to be deprogrammed.

In retrospect, the programming was one of the most difficult things for Yael to deal with. There was a persistence about my terror, and an insistence about what was still going to happen to me, that was not simply the result of abuse. Whenever Yael could identify that this was the result of programming, she helped me see what was real and what wasn't, but like everything else, it took a long time for me to register that the reality of my abuse was over.

chapter 22

Raven, Hate, and Fuckface on the Road to Integration

As Ruthie and Lili grew, their natures stayed the same. Lili acted out physically and I responded in kind. Ruthie, frequently Lili's target, buried her emotions. She read voraciously to escape the chaos, and filled notebook after notebook with writings that, despite her anguish and loneliness, were preternaturally beautiful. With the help of therapists, doctors, teachers, medication, and time, Lili improved and had fewer tantrums, but I still responded roughly. I was desperately trying to navigate and rein in my angry alters, but I was never fast enough.

Raven, Hate, and Fuckface, who had been without my conscious awareness for many years, became emboldened. They identified with my abusers and, like them, were cruel and evil. My work with Yael triggered them, and so did Susie's increasing impatience, Lili's dysregulated behavior, and Ruthie's quiet need for attention. Often lost in this was Flannery, now an adult yet still with her own conflicts and need for mothering.

For many months, I wondered where *my* anger was. Although Hate tried to come out early on, he was not able to relate well. I was rarely combative in my sessions and I was not a characteristically angry person. Or so I thought. In fact, I was raging at home with Susie and the girls all the time. If I wasn't spaced out or dissociated as a young part, I was furious and unaware of it. As I wrote and journaled, I learned that this part who could speak was Raven. From the time I first became aware of this member of the gang, I tried desperately to get rid of him. I wrote:

Was in many places today, but the angry, acting-out grown-up is banging around + furious. He does not belong, he is done, finished. We have no use for him. No surprise he is not going without a battle. Way too arrogant to admit defeat. It's fucking over. You are toxic, hateful, manipulative, disgusting. You have zero self-control, no morals, you like to fuck and fuck over. So now you are getting fucked by the rest of us. I don't ever want to talk about you anymore. Drop dead.

With Yael's insight, it became clear that Hate, Raven, and Fuckface were imprints of Jack and my abusers living inside of me. Creating an alter who can be like your abuser, who can predict what is going to happen to you next, can be lifesaving, but living with this part once the abuse is over is horrific.

What I came to believe through my therapy is that communication between parts is essential to healing. That meant I had to talk (not out loud!) to my parts as if they were individual people and listen to them as well.

Raven, Hate, and Fuckface . . .

I couldn't get rid of parts that I didn't like; I could only hear them, listen to what they were trying to tell me, and perhaps give them other jobs to perform in my new healthier state. Banishing them was not a possibility. Meanwhile, Raven frightened me and anyone else he encountered. Yael and I tried for many months to get him to come out during a session, but he was not having any part of it. One morning I woke up and found this on my computer:

IT IS FUCKING RIDICULOUS TO THINK THAT I WILL TELL YOU ANYTHING SINCE MOST OF THE TIME I THINK ABOUT DE-STROYING YOUR OFFICE AND BODY SLAMMING YOU UNCON-SCIOUS. I WOULD LOVE NOTHING BETTER THAN TO FIGHT WITH YOU OVER CONTROL OF THE GANG. THERE IS NO WAY THIS SYSTEM CAN SURVIVE IF I AM TAMED OR KILLED OFF OR EVEN GIVEN A NEW JOB. DANGER IS EVERYWHERE AND IT IS CONSTANT. IT COMES IN MANY FORMS BUT THE BOTTOM LINE IS THAT WE ARE WIRED TO SELF-DESTRUCT IF TRIG-GERED AND WILL BECOME VIOLENT IF AN ATTEMPT IS MADE TO STOP US. SHELLEY HAS TOLD ME THAT YOU ARE NOT CONCERNED ABOUT YOUR SAFETY WHICH IS UNWISE TO SAY THE LEAST. DON'T FORGET THAT THE SAME STRENGTH THAT IS SUMMONED TO STAY ALIVE IS USED TO HURT OTH-ERS. YOU ARE A MAIN TARGET OF COURSE, SINCE YOU NOW HOLD SO MUCH INFORMATION THAT HAS PREVIOUSLY BEEN SECRETED BY THE CULT. WHAT YOU DON'T KNOW IS HOW THEY WENT ABOUT BREAKING THE LITTLE ONES DOWN BUT I CAN TELL YOU AND IT REALLY WAS A PERFECT SYS-TEM. IT ALWAYS STARTED WITH LOVE, COMFORT, SAFETY.

Raven, Hate, and Fuckface . . .

THEN JUST A LITTLE STRESS TO GET A LITTLE CONFLICT
ALIVE. SMILES AND RESPONSE WERE ENCOURAGED, REIN-
FORCED AND TOLERATED. THEY WERE EXPECTED. UNTIL
THEY WEREN'T ANY LONGER. THEN THE PUNISHMENTS BE-
GAN—STRANGLING

Holy shit! I considered a quick delete but I recognized that Raven was speaking to me and I needed to listen. Although it was not news to me, I felt Raven's fury in all of its power and it was indeed frightening. Knowing that I had written it without remembering was disturbing at best. Raven continued to wreak havoc in my life and not understanding a lot of the havoc as it happened was infuriating. I was still not aware of my splitting at home, only during my sessions with Yael. Even then, I often did not remember what I had done or said. DID fascinated me but at the same time, I felt so distraught that I remained suicidal off and on for years. I could not accept that I said terrible things to Susie and my kids or was rough with Lili.

Whenever Susie tried to tell me what I had said or done, I became angry and disconnected and did not believe her. She could not be describing *me*—I had no memory of this behavior. Hearing about it left me confused and depressed and terrified that I would never get well. It left her equally confused and enraged. We had abandoned our couples therapy and so she had nowhere to put her anger and frustration. Sometimes she came to see Yael with me, which triggered me to dissociate in the sessions and insist that Susie was the one with the problems. I could not stand having another person in the room when I was with Yael. That was *my* space and I had a hard time sharing it. I could not hear or accept that I was abusive at home and it was years until I was able to see this part in action and stop it.

It was even longer before I appreciated that Raven was protecting me and that harnessing his rage was not only possible but beneficial to the gang.

Email to Yael

I am a mess, churning inside and angry, disconnected. Whatever arousal I had is long gone and I am left feeling raped and left to die.

I also wonder, like you, about the benefit of remembering, and am aware more than ever of how re-traumatizing it is to go back.

at the same time, I am getting better—that is certain—and I don't think that remembering is without any merit. I think and I hope I am right, that this link between abuse and arousal and need for nurturing, along with my sadness and shame, is the epicenter behind my symptoms. I guess I will always doubt that my need for you to take care of me will ever subside, since so often I feel like a baby falling backward though the sky. But I have to believe I will grow up and out of such desperate need, or I would give up already. Tommy was in agony today. But he is letting you in, ever so slowly, and even he knows how good that feels. I will keep thinking about untangling my brain.

It took three years to get to know most of my parts and the abuse they endured. Therapy was a relentless march through memories and trauma, with not much of a break. To make matters worse, I was reminded daily of how vulnerable Lili and Ruthie were at their present age of seven. I could not fathom them enduring a rape, let alone never being able to talk about it. All these years into therapy I remained sleepless and anorectic yet was now gradually seeing glimmers of light. There were good days mixed with bad ones, but the trend was thankfully toward recovery.

Raven, Hate, and Fuckface . . .

EMAIL TO YAEL

so here is the way I see it.

there was the process of remembering the abuse so that I could recognize and give context to all of my parts. lots of abreacting, lots of trauma.

there is the process of getting to know all the parts, what they need, where they came from and what they can do next. lots of thinking, not so much abreacting, lots of reacting.

there is life which causes me to dissociate at times, to abreact at other times, and pushes me to understand my triggers

there is my relationship with you which allows all of this to happen. neither life nor relationships are linear and so there will be times when one or both of us wonders why is this happening, why the memory, why now, when will this phase end?

and I say, who the fuck knows? it's working though. and I love you for that.

I was so happy to have the abreactions fading that I was slammed and completely unprepared when it came time to begin to integrate my parts. Despite my hopes, it was neither a relief, a resolution, nor an easy process. In addition, there was shame to deal with, as I recalled the many times I was told I was disgusting and bad by the cult.

EMAIL TO YAEL

You know it is easier for me to remember being tortured than to deal with my shame. It is the most sickening and pervasive and depressing state imaginable. And each time it hits, it absolutely stuns me, as if poison was released into my bloodstream and I am simply waiting to die. I don't know how to get to original shame, but it sure would be nice to exorcise it.

chapter 23

Tommy Fragments

———

Tommy was one of my most prominent and complicated alters and he had an exceedingly difficult time in therapy, having witnessed much of the original abuse, taken care of the little ones along the way, and watched all of the abreactions and healing take place. He didn't want any part of it. As a boy, he was unwilling to talk through things and unable to express much emotion; he was locked up. And as protective as he was, he was also furious about the abuse and the consequent fallout years later. Yael and I had recognized that Tommy was a multiple himself, with his own younger parts and a fierce Denier of his own who kept Yael at a distance for several years.

Tommy was making progress with EMDR and began hypnosis, since he was adamant that he not abreact or cry during his recovery. He wrote to Yael:

I have a few questions about hypnosis.
Are we starting tomorrow?

Tommy Fragments

Do I have to keep my eyes closed the whole time?

Will I be sitting in the chair (those chairs suck for relaxing)?

Are you going to touch me? It's ok I think if you do

Is anyone else allowed to speak

Am I going to remember everything?

How long will I be hypnotized?

Do you think I'm a multiple? I don't want to be.

Tommy

We tried it. It was not an instant success; nothing was instant at all during any part of therapy.

EMAIL TO YAEL

I am so sad and frustrated and angry. I was feeling so good. Not even disconnected from the reality of my past. I felt like I had turned a corner. And in all honesty, I was kind of excited about hypnosis, about tommy being ready to do his thing, to heal, to deal, etc.

Now I want to go in a corner and hide. Hypnosis may be a good way to find out stuff, but it doesn't leave me feeling any better than a full-blown abreaction. Maybe worse because I feel a little like I've always felt when moving from one state to another. Kind of dazed, confused, disconnected and also sad, deeply sad.

I suppose that I needed a little more time to process whatever came up, and although chatting about life, movies, the Oscars, helped me to be in the present with you, there was no there there. I was still in some murky past place that I knew was horrible, but I couldn't touch the feelings that were part of that past. Just like it was then, really. There but not there, in pain but not feeling it, speaking the unspeakable and not being connected to it.

Also, it was a fucking lot of work. Poor Tommy's brain was fried by the end. It felt like he had just taken his SAT's in Chinese. It all gave me a big headache.

So, hey let's do it again tomorrow! Seriously, you know me and change—when I'm ready for it there is no stopping me. And I certainly did think I was ready. Maybe it was too much too fast. There was little of the old familiar us today and that made me sad. But mostly I feel like we opened something up again. And maybe we did and maybe that's the point and maybe tommy needs to do it this way. who the fuck knows? I am so tired of living with this stuff and feeling like every time I get a little taste of life I get sucked back down into the black hole of my past.

It wasn't just Tommy—all my parts needed individual therapy of some sort. The little ones colored and drew pictures and talked about what had happened. Seven remained depressed and unreachable for years. Yael often said Seven might never heal, that she was unable to trust anyone enough to come into her inner world.

EMAIL TO YAEL

Seven is still waiting to cry. She is used to time going slowly for her—she always feels like things are in slow motion, but now she blames Tommy for not helping her get to a point where she can grieve and move on. And I think that she feels that they need to close that memory together. She thinks that if he came out in the first place to handle the rape, then he should be able to deal with it. He feels that he can get angry but not sad, she feels the opposite. I think they are right that they need to resolve it together.

Peanut is seeing their struggle and is identifying in spades. She was split off from Shelley and she split to have sex with Alice sometimes when Tommy took over. It seems that they each need to cooperate to feel whole, since nothing that happened involved only one of them, and each violation elicited more than one emotion.

Peanut had to keep going back over her memories because she felt responsible for everything that happened with Alice and she couldn't shake the shame. She was also confused because she loved Alice, despite her recognition that what happened between them was wrong. Butch/Romeo was most aligned with Peanut, and in fact, might have been Peanut grown up. They were all able to relate to each other about their obsession with sex and their belief that it was synonymous with love.

Butch/Romeo remained my most poorly behaved alter. Even years into therapy, they were unwilling to come into the room and do serious work toward healing. Their language was sexual, and it was impossible for them to either abreact or just talk. They knew on some level that their actions were meant to cover the pain of my abuse, but they could not change, and I needed them to. Lastly, the shame associated with sex in general made them self-loathing, which made it difficult for me to deal with them, as long as I was still dissociated. During this phase of therapy, I was getting to know all my parts better so that they could be integrated, but Butch/Romeo were holding out so much that I remained obsessional, and more importantly, vulnerable.

Tommy Fragments

Although they had not acted out since my relationship with Susie began, in 2011, after four years of therapy, that kind of changed.

chapter 24

The Grief of Lost Time

Now that some of the younger alters had been recognized and cared for, I decided to return to the Fresh Meadows house to see if I could shake anything loose in my already cacophonous brain. I had visited there ten years earlier when Carol was still my therapist and I had discovered the basement was identical to the one in the drawings I'd shared with her, complete with ladder and dangling light bulb, but I never really walked the property or looked inside the house.

I felt brave back then, but this time around I was terrified.

I guess because I now knew that everything I had drawn or written about or remembered was real and true. I wanted Yael to go with me and she was happy to do so. My gang was less enthusiastic about the trip—they went nuts at the prospect and spent weeks agitated about what we were all going to experience. We all dreaded a collision—the integration of psychic pain between different alters.

It seems that many of my parts needed to merge and share

their pain with other parts and what resulted was a collision. During colli-sions I experienced deafeningly painful episodes that I was told were even more painful to watch than to endure. I sat screaming on the floor, hold-ing my head for fear that it would explode. This was the piece of the inte-gration process I hated and dreaded the most. It felt like a bad acid trip. Each part brought its full complement of pain and as they collided, their pain was exchanged, shared, and consequently dissipated. These collisions were most disturbing for Yael, who felt I was experiencing a cerebral stroke or some original torturous pain. That was about right. Afterward, I be-came spaced out and calm and I knew that some pain had been exorcised. When I think back over my years in therapy, I don't remember a lot of abreactions, but I remember every collision.

EMAIL TO YAEL

interesting assortment of parts coming out today. it is kind of funny (and not so much) that they all feel entitled to communicate with you without checking with the others. for someone who thinks things to death and obsesses about relationships, this is pretty unusual/strange brave/liberating/disconcerting.

at any rate Seven seems to be jockeying for some attention. I would imagine that she is quite apprehensive about her upcoming field trip and doesn't feel entitled to have a reaction because she never lived there. We are all dreading a Little Girl/Seven/Peanut collision and kind of assume that it will not happen outside of your office. but I guess we are not sure of that, which is adding to our anxiety. collisions are already so painful and the thought of having one at "the scene of" feels utterly raw. but i guess there is nothing to do about it anyway.

Tommy is also dreading the trip and is afraid that he will finally feel too fragmented to recover. Although he has accepted his multiplicity at times, he pretty much stays in denial that he was really there. Interestingly, he does not seem to have much difficulty believing that everything happened, he just doesn't fully believe that it happened to him. He doesn't see that after Little Girl created him, he then split into the other boys and was much in the middle of everything bad. His guilt is even greater than Joey's and Malcolm's since he believes that he was old enough to know better and big enough to not be bullied into action. He is also anxious about Seven being there since she will remind him of the rape in Connecticut which so far is his worst memory ever. His whole being feels threatened and scared and his ability to drive Shelley feels not just diminished but eliminated.

Raven doesn't know what to think, not being much of a thinker to begin with. As with all the boys, he is not a natural at understanding his actions, both past and present. But at least in the past, he could stay disconnected enough to avoid feeling anything but rage. Now he feels afraid and broken and homeless and isn't sure if and when that rage will come back and how he will express it.

Aimee wants to see the inside of the Watkins house and Little Girl doesn't. Little Girl has been warned about seeing the basement under the Watkins house and Tommy and Five do not want to go there. They are all afraid that the dead cat will still be there along with some knives. B/R are a little like Tommy in that they don't believe they were there. I'm not sure what they are feeling and honestly don't even know if they will come. They do seem to get that this is not a fun or sexy trip.

And so, we went. Yael drove, mostly because I wasn't sure I would be

The Grief of Lost Time

able to drive myself home. We wandered into the backyard, passing the entrance to the basement, and I seemed fine. I was feeling scientific about the whole thing—gathering data for a study on my life. It was as if time stood still—almost everything was as it had been some fifty-two years before, including the same slide in the middle of the playground. There was not a living soul to be seen and the place felt a little haunted. Yael and I sat there quietly for some time. I pointed out our house and the Watkinses' and showed Yael the entrance to the basement. I looked up at the window on the second floor where Jack orally raped Little Girl while the bright sun illuminated the room.

Yael and I left without knocking on any doors or seeing inside the apartments as I knew I would not handle that well. We went down the road and had ice cream and chatted. I was a little dissociated but I told Yael that I could take the subway back into the city. I had expected fireworks and explosions but got a sparkler instead. Nonetheless, the visit to Fresh Meadows allowed me to feel the grief of lost time.

chapter 25

Enduring Sorrow

I had never experienced grief as I did during my recovery. It was a dark black hole, cloyingly close like the dampness of a cellar. Once I felt it, it could be retrieved more easily; often when I didn't want it. When I was mourning, there was no room for anything or anyone else. Sometimes I cycled in and out, remembering for a moment that life was going on but then not feeling like I wanted to be a part of it.

There were so many reasons to grieve. I could not count them. I never really had a chance at a normal life, at innocence, at being loved and cared for—I was whisked away while still in diapers and I was tortured. I understood death in a primitive way, since death really meant nothing to me then, but the feeling of falling unattended, of enduring pain that was horrific and seemingly endless, was the first death I knew. I wished that memories would stop, but I also wished that *I* would stop—both could accomplish the same goal. I grieved for that earliest sense of safety, for the unconditional love of a caregiver.

Enduring Sorrow

As I grew older—and by "older," I mean three or four years of age—I did not know peace, I did not know innocence. And I did not know childhood. I was always waiting for the next round of bad things to happen; waiting for the pain, the loneliness, the lack of protection. My early childhood was stripped of discovery and wonder. What replaced it was truly devastating to my soul, and so I grieved for the childhood that was taken from me.

I did not have a mother who knew how to love. She was an immature narcissist and her children were not only ornaments, but also used to obtain attention and love that she craved. Neither my brother nor I was loved in that selfless way that warms your body and soul. We were left to find that elsewhere, and we never really did. And the safest and most important caregiver and protector in my young life permitted me to be tortured and violated: I mourned the mother I never had.

There are too many years between then and now to even fathom the degree of grief in my life. My teen years were rampant with neglect, which set me up as prey for someone like my coach. The seeds were sown and the utter despair from a life of limited love and attention was deeper than the heart could endure. All the good that has come my way since was built on this foundation, a layer that feels neither strong nor resilient. Now any human suffering or anything that suggests loss resonates with that crumbling layer of despair. Since Yael urged me to cry, something that I fought for many years and loathed for as many, I now cry constantly. Movies, the news, commercials, watching my kids fight, my patients' sorrow—anything that *could* bring tears does. And they are not the gentle, rolling-over-your-eyelid tears or the welling-up variety. They are sobbing-from-the-depths tears and there are many more to shed.

Enduring Sorrow

I don't know if the well ever dries or if the flow diminishes. I don't know what happens when you add new real-life grief to the grief that is yet to be unburdened. Probably some of the old gets rekindled and feels fresh again. Maybe they merge and they sit together in that dark hole. Maybe grief gets recycled but is never fully gone. At worst, I will take some of it to the grave with me. At best, I will carry only a portion of it, which I assume is normal, since life and loss are forever interconnected.

chapter 26

Sickness and Health

In August 2010, I experienced a new kind of grief when Susie found a large lump in her left breast. Her mammogram from one and a half years earlier had been normal but we were still worried. Her grandmother had had a double mastectomy, and this fueled our fears. On the other hand, cancer happened to other people, not us. The girls were seven; old enough to understand, and young enough to just wonder.

I immediately called my friend Deborah, who is a breast surgeon. She was out of town, dropping her son off at college in North Carolina, but she saw Susie the day she returned. She did a needle aspiration in the office and the pathologist read it immediately. It was cancer. We were quiet. Not too many questions. She wanted Susie to have tests to determine if there was any metastatic disease and they would operate in a few weeks' time.

I checked out.

I mostly thought I was present and supportive and helpful,

but I was none of these things. I did not accompany Susie to any of her tests, my excuse being that I could not cancel appointments with patients. I began socializing with some doctors, including her breast surgeon, her oncologists, and a few others. Despite Susie having been a part of the group from the start, when the day came for our first group dinner, I told Susie I didn't want her to be there. This hurt her, big time. And so when we all got together, I *talked* about Susie and therefore believed that I was being attentive. In truth, I was greatly enjoying my independence from her and from the cancer that terrified me.

Illness, vulnerability, and loss involving someone who was supposed to ground and protect me all drove me away and I dissociated easily. I was afraid of being left and so I left first. One of the oncologists—Jane—was fast becoming a friend. Too fast. She was straight and divorced with two kids, and yet she was flirting with me and I with her. Butch/Romeo was out and working hard to protect me from my fears of abandonment. Whenever I saw Yael, she would ask me if anything was going on. I told her the truth, which was that nothing was happening but that Jane was flirting with me and denying it. I also said that I was not interested in her. Yael warned me of the slippery slope of attraction and I felt that if I brought what was happening into our session, I would be okay. My "affair" with Jane was an intensely emotional one that lasted six months, and was just as hurtful to Susie as if we had slept together.

———————

Meanwhile, Susie had bilateral mastectomies and reconstruction. She had no metastases. I was pretty much absent the whole time. I was there for her post-op in body but not so much in spirit. I was a total asshole, but in all fairness to myself, I was completely dissociated, something I couldn't control.

I had always remembered the mutilation of a young woman by the cult and Susie, in equal measure, was now mutilated as well. I was unable to keep things separate. Susie, in the meantime, underwent twelve weeks of chemotherapy followed by twenty-eight rounds of radiation, and I did not accompany her to any of her treatments. Amy, our irreplaceable friend, stepped in and took care of her. Amy was aware of my DID in a way that not too many people were at the time. She supported Susie 100 percent, shared (or perhaps absorbed) her anger and pain, and managed somehow not to judge me. The kids saw her as their "third mom." Because I was absent and Susie was dealing with the side effects of her treatment, Amy would gather our two girls along with her own kids and take everyone to the movies, miniature golf, or the park. She kept our family sane and I will never understand how she managed to do it, but that's just Amy.

Sometime after Susie's chemo, but before her radiation, I began bleeding. Being sixty and long done with periods, I had a workup and found I would need a hysterectomy in a few months. This was not good timing. My general position on medical problems is that you deal with them alone. You do not take anyone with you to the doctor, and you do not acknowledge pain of any sort, emotional or physical. For this I was well trained, but I had young parts who were frightened and needed support. I grudgingly let Susie take care of me but was unpleasant to her throughout the ordeal.

My monstrous behavior did not just begin when I learned that I had DID, but between then and the aftermath of Susie's breast cancer diagnosis, our relationship was strained beyond all reason. We were the classic couple who stayed together for the children, although we did love each other deeply. My behavior became increasingly difficult to bear once I was in the throes of memories and recovery. That is when my meanest parts emerged, and Susie received the lion's share of my ugliness. She was severely tested by my relationship with Yael—its intensity, intimacy, and primacy. She understood DID as well as anyone who doesn't have it can, but my frustration with her intolerance of my splitting was great. I kept her in the dark a lot, because I was too vulnerable to share the process with her, afraid she would somehow use it against me.

As understandable as all of this was, it made for significant stress between us at a time when we both needed one another a great deal. I asked Susie to text or email me every time she felt I was dissociating at home and saying things that were particularly malicious. This would give me a written account of things I didn't remember saying or doing. It took a long time for her to get into the habit of doing this, in part because it was exhausting and in part because I would tell her in the most loathsome way that she didn't have to bother writing since I was aware of what I had said.

I wasn't.

Days or weeks later when she told me something I had done or said and I was able to hear her, I became distraught, depressed, and often suicidal. The reality of my living this other life and not knowing it was too much for me to bear. Being as controlling a person as I was yet not having any control whatsoever was enraging and disheartening at best.

A dark cloud hovered over me for many weeks and I tried to work harder in therapy. Yael explained over and over that I could not help dissociating, but I became angry and frustrated and then just wanted to give up. I didn't feel that I could get better quickly enough to hold on to my family.

I was ashamed. And when shame blankets you, there is nothing worse—it contaminates your soul and makes you want to disappear into death. It is virtually impossible to shake and lingers for a long time.

I am still not the best person to be around when Susie feels ill or vulnerable. One of my most devastating cult memories was the sacrifice of a baby girl who I thought was killed because she was crying. I was told and then programmed to believe that *any* vulnerability on my part would mean death for me as it had for that little girl. As an adult, my fear of losing Susie combined with my identification with the aggressor, a hallmark characteristic of DID, resulted in my contempt for Susie when she was hurting or crying or sick. The irony that I am a doctor and that I always empathize with my patients is not lost on me.

It wasn't lost on my wife either—she rightfully deserved some of that compassion when she was not well. I still, even now, must work on being kinder to her. I have to remind myself to be empathetic and sensitive. Often this means talking to Fuckface. Yet it is still awkward for me to do so. The forces inside my DID head are extraordinary. Sometimes all the voices talk at the same time, and the result is ambivalence, or more severely, paralysis. It is not until I recognize and communicate with each part that I am able to tame them. It is truly a miracle the way the mind works and an even bigger miracle that Susie stood by me through all of this.

chapter 27

Collisions and Aftershock

My father had Alzheimer's. We watched him deteriorate over the years and thought he was dying several times when he didn't. It's a devastating disease and I'm sure that he would not have wanted to live the way he did in his final years. He could barely walk, he was in a diaper, and he couldn't remember much of anything. When he was still a little cognizant, I remember talking with him about my DID. He was truly empathic and kind of fascinated. He wanted to know more, and he asked if I could email him my thoughts. I felt that I might finally be heard by at least one parent. I spent a good amount of time writing him an email that explained my parts and how they all worked together.

After I sent the email, my father never responded. When I visited him, he did not remember reading it. I can't say I was heartbroken, but I was incredibly sad. The disease had ravaged his beautiful mind. He remained sweet most of the time—at least he was to me—and would light up whenever I came to see him. He loved seeing his grandchildren and when urged, would tell them stories about his life. But this all came to an end in his last year, and when we finally had to get him an aide, it was as if he was lost forever. One day, he went into the hospital with back pain. A CT scan showed a large abdominal tumor. It was an aggressive lymphoma and we made the decision to put him in hospice. He was dead three days later.

He died one month after Susie's mastectomies. I was in Connecticut on and off for several weeks and Susie was recovering on her own. I distanced myself from my terror about losing Susie, but loss was nevertheless not far away from me. My brother Bob and I handled everything together and got along superbly. We had no funeral but sat shiva for two nights and people came from all over to pay their respects. Colleagues and secretaries and friends alike spoke of Dad's generosity and fairness, his humor and intellect; the stories were endless but lovely. Cards flowed in with such glowing accounts that at one point my mother asked, "Are they talking about your father?"

Although he had been a fairly sexist guy, he was more of a parent to me than my mother ever was. He always expected me to excel in both sports and academics. He played ball and shot hoops with me and was proud of my athleticism. Tommy adored him and did not do well after his death. All my parts got stirred up and I leaned heavily, as always, on Yael.

I wrote to Yael that Tommy was not taking care of the little ones and was having his own crisis. The gang fractured all over again. Parts that Tommy had created—Raven and Fuckface—had been pushing for a collision and my father's death caused them to have one. It was horrendous, physically and emotionally, as if Raven was killing me in the process.

EMAIL TO YAEL

Collisions. I have told you that I think they represent the integration of psychic pain coming from different parts. Although I dissociated from physical pain, I'm not really sure what I did with psychic pain. It feels like it came later for each part, that it got buried even deeper and became less accessible. It feels more unbearable than physical pain since it does not have a beginning and an end. Without that arc, it seems truly endless, and in fact, although the physical pain did end, the psychic pain did not. Somehow, the process of coping with both feels different. Re-experiencing psychic pain is not visual, although the initial collision is. I can always see each part before they collide, and I am aware at that moment that neither part has really accepted or embraced the other's existence. The collision seems to generate enough energy to release the pain and bring it into consciousness where it can be seen, heard, and felt by me, and more importantly, by you. Once both of us have seen it and felt it, I can then integrate it and own it. For each collision, the pain comes to the surface and becomes part of my conscious fabric. It also fights with denier for control of the moment and for the truth of my past. It is as essential if not more so than the memories, for it is the last layer.

You asked me this last time what you can do, what do I need or want when I am colliding. You have always done the right thing, so I think you know already. I have to feel supremely safe to go there, which I do. I have to feel like I will not die in the process, and that my pain does not frighten or overwhelm you. It is a delicate balance for you to react to and absorb that pain without my feeling that it will overwhelm you. But however you have managed so far, it has come through to me that you are stronger than they were, and that your love will extinguish the pain in time. I cannot ask for more and you could not give me more. I know that you are feeling helpless at the time, but in fact, your presence is what allows me to go there and it is what allows me to fully feel that last layer so that I can move on. I also know that it is harder to watch than to experience, because for me it is cathartic—it is important for you to know that.

Email to Yael

Mostly I think I am so exhausted from being a grown-up, and now I have added my mother as yet another person to take care of. It is amazing how happy she is to depend upon me, and puzzling why I take care of her so well. Even on the phone with you, I needed to be a grown-up, and I guess that finished me off.

I'm not sure if the little ones need more attention than usual, or just some for a change. With Tommy in a state of I'm not sure what, they are particularly stranded. I'm not even 100% sure how I know that he is off, but I do. I feel so lost beneath the surface—there is no "there" there. Voices and parts are rumbling around, kind of looking for some order, and so so sad that Tommy seems gone.

We all continued along, trying to grieve, trying to take care of Susie and Lili and Ruthie and my mother, and trying to get my parts back together so that they could work in some cooperative fashion. About a month after my father's death, the pain finally provoked a collision in Yael's office. It was between Tommy and Raven.

oh that was so painful today.

and sad. in fact, heart-wrenching.

I don't know how many more collisions I can withstand, but not too many more with raven. Usually collisions are so much more in my head than in my body. They always feel like some explosion of psychic pain, but today was more physically painful and psychically terrifying because it felt like raven was killing me with his beak and claws and smothering me in his wings. it was like a bad trip. I'm glad you were blocking my fall today because I thought that he was going to throw me to the floor and destroy me.

meanwhile, I don't really know how you do it but I'm glad you do. I am still stunned by how much trust is in that room, but let me tell you, from my perspective, it is not only necessary but it is life-affirming. Even when evil is pummeling me, you are there, and you are steady. And when three four five parts come out in a session, though it nauseates me, it must mean that everyone is wanting to heal. Otherwise, why bother, really?

A few months after my dad died, I received a condolence card from Jack Watkins' oldest daughter. It came to my office. When I saw her name in the return address, I was apoplectic. I stared at the envelope for a long time before I opened it, simultaneously dreading and looking for affirmation of my abuse. After reading the contents, I was massively messed up. I must have thrown the card out in an unusual moment of fury, so what I write here is unfortunately limited.

Collisions and Aftershock

I had not seen her since I was four years old and had not heard from her since then either. We did play together when we were neighbors, and my parents made quite an impression on her. What she said made my head spin. She wrote briefly about my dad, sending her condolences, and then moved on to my mom. She remembered her with great fondness. According to her, my mother babysat for them when her own mom went into the hospital to deliver her younger sister. She described how small my mother looked in her parents' bed and how cute she was. She also rambled on about her own life, described her own dad as kind and funny, and ended with a confession about how depressed and anxious she was as an adult.

This was written by a woman in her mid-sixties to, essentially, a stranger.

I had many questions. Why was my mother in Jack and Virginia's bed? Why was Jack's daughter writing to me after all these years? Why did she feel it necessary to talk about how great her own dad was? And all of this without talking about my father, for whom she supposedly had written the note in the first place. I tried not to get deeply psychoanalytical and stuck to the facts of her letter. More importantly, I showed the letter to Susie, Yael, and a few friends to try to get some objective feedback. They all felt the same way: this was bizarre. Their reactions were unequivocal.

I will never know what went on in her head as she wrote to me; I can only deduce things from the content. The single most interesting fact was that my mother stayed overnight in their bed. *Why?* Much later I came to remember that my mother and Jack had been sexual and were sleeping together. But why was his daughter, now in her mid-sixties, telling me this with the innocence of a child? And why was she so forthcoming about her own mental problems?

None of my analysis is all that important; what matters is what it stirred up in me. Yael agreed that the card was deeply disturbing on so many levels and anticipated that my response would include paranoia that they were still coming after me. This was programmed into me repeatedly—that they would always know where I was and would always be able to "get me." Yael had to remind my little ones that Jack and Virginia Watkins were indeed dead, that the abuse was over, and that nothing in the future would happen to me because of them.

She wrote to me that night:

First of all, I want to say that you could have done without ever hearing from any Watkins EVER and I am sorry that you have to relive it AGAIN as a result of it. Of course it would feel threatening in some way, especially for the little ones who were told that these ugly fuckers (I think that may be my new name for them, with your permission) would always find you. It sent chills up my spine, so it makes total sense that it took all week for it to slowly hit you. DAMN THEM.

Sadness is one of those forbidden emotions that was tortured out of you at such a young age. Even feeling your sadness for a moment feels so deeply despairing that it can only be tolerated a bit at a time. That's why I think I understand what you mean about affirmation with no denial feels like death. It truly feels unsurvivable...if you did not split off to share all the pain. Each one of your parts created to survive the abuse had more pain than any one person should have in one lifetime. Who can believe that one person, one beating heart, one soul can endure such UNIMAGINABLE horror for every minute of those first years of life? And still remain loving and kind and giving, and and and...you are remarkable beyond belief. And you are getting better. A lot better.

chapter 28

Trust and Denial

There were a lot of things going on at the beginning of 2011. Dad had just died and Tommy was bereft. So
were the others. Susie was in the throes of chemotherapy and
I was having an extremely difficult time being supportive. Yael
was admitted to the hospital several times with acute asthma.
And lastly, my brother and I had to take care of my mother, the
parent I had come to distrust and dislike.

All of my parts were reacting, but Tommy was especially
angry and lost and didn't quite know how to deal with his grief
or his multiplicity. He tried at times to come out in sessions,
but he often did so at the end when Yael had no time to talk
with him or so briefly that she didn't know he was there. After
one such session, he wrote:

EMAIL TO YAEL

*are you fucking kidding me? this is why I don't come out
much anymore 'cause there is no way that we can get any-*

thing done. I watch you with the others and you are different. I'm done.

tommy

EMAIL FROM YAEL

Dear Tommy,

Wow. That took me by surprise. So I don't know everything and I don't always have your number.

Can you help me understand what upset you? I appreciate the feedback because I think we can find a way to work together and get things done.

I am sure that I am different with the little ones, both because they are little, and therefore simpler, and also because you are a teen boy and frankly, I don't completely get teen boys. I want to, so I have to know what pisses you off and what works for you. I promise to be completely honest with you in return. I love you in the same way I love the little ones—I may not be as good at showing it to you, but I will work on it. Thanks, tommy.

Tommy had begun to accept his parts, especially after Seven's memory of her rape. He struggled with his role as manager, as it was a tremendous burden for him to take care of the gang and himself. It was similar to how I felt having to take care of Susie and the kids and provide for them.

EMAIL FROM TOMMY TO YAEL

I am in a murderous rage, am sitting on a shitload of anger, trying to keep all these fucking voices clear and trying to deliver them to you in some order that makes sense. I don't even know what any of them are going to say anymore even though supposedly I'm in charge. and we will never get done because I will never tell you really how I'm feeling. mostly because I don't really always know what I'm feeling and also, since you are a girl and not a guy you can't really help me figure it out. when guys figure out what they are feeling which is never easy, the last thing that they want to do is share that with our mom which is what most girls are. they're our moms. we love them but we hate them. they have everything that we want and we can't have any part of them except the mom part but once we are teenagers that feels too dangerous and confusing, and moms feel it too. They get all sweet and cuddly and gentle with you when you're little and then they pull away. So we are left on our own to figure things out and to do it on our own when we are way too young to be on our own. and especially if we're hurt and shamed and we need to feel better, well there is no way to get what we need. and so we get pissy and cranky and horny and we jerk off and drive fast and say mean things so that we don't have to feel close and frustrated anymore. so if you ask me what happened yesterday I'm not even sure I could tell you. I know that seven was getting what she needed finally and I should have felt good about that but I couldn't help thinking that she's not the only one who got raped but she doesn't want to rape back and I do and I hate everyone so much that I want to kill everybody in sight. I feel sick inside with hate and it sits there rotting me and then it comes out sometimes I'm not expecting it and pow, there is all this rage and I don't know if I want to kill or cry or get laid and I think that crying might feel good 'cause as soon as I got your email I started to cry 'cause you were so nice and I didn't really want to hurt you but I didn't

Trust and Denial

know what else to do with all those feelings. and asking for help is kind of impossible because that vulnerable feeling makes me feel like I will never have any control left which is kind of like dying and I don't know what you would do or say but I can't really get held 'cause then I would feel too close and confused and I can't really sit there and cry because it feels so lonely and painful so it's easier to shut down. So I came out in the room yesterday thinking well maybe I could get taken care of too and that was so brave of me only it was too late and I had to go back inside right away as our session was ending which felt humiliating and it convinced me that I needed to be alone with all those feelings and that's the way it is.

and the worst part was that you met little tommy yesterday and he seemed to feel fine coming out and he could tell in your eyes that you thought he was kind of cute and you NEVER think I'm cute but you are sort of intrigued with me but I'm needing love and a mom and for someone to say that I don't need to hold everyone and everything together anymore and maybe I could come unglued and it would be ok and then I could start to put all the pieces back together but maybe with some help this time. I don't know if this is making any sense at all but I hope so 'cause then maybe you could help me. And you're gonna say that I should go hit a baseball or a punching bag or ride my bike or climb a tree but I'm telling you that that is not gonna deal with the rage and that rage is scaring me so much mostly cause I never felt it like this before.

So I am sorry that I said such mean shit to you cause you didn't really do anything to deserve it and even if you did I don't really want to be mean to you cause you're trying to help me.

Since Tommy had created Raven and Fuckface, his anger was now being expressed by these alters, and he was feeling every bit of their rage and paranoia. He worked extremely hard with Yael to unburden these feelings; it remained a difficult and painful undertaking for him. He processed much of this in his emails to Yael.

EMAIL FROM TOMMY TO YAEL

I have asked Writer to help me explain some things because my writing can get kind of run-on and then is hard to understand. I'm not sure if Writer is a boy or a girl or both, but I'm pretty sure that we can work together.

I think you know—I know that you know—how hard this week was for me. It began two Fridays ago and I have to say that even I was surprised by the depth of my rage. The gang has left your office so many times feeling frustrated, unfinished, needy—those are the times they think they could stay there forever and would never fill up the hole that lives inside them. But they do leave, and remarkably, carry on. They get distracted or busy or simply enough time passes for the emptiness to be forgotten. They have also gotten angry—angry that you waited too long to let them recover, angry that one of them didn't get to come out, angry that you had a life away from them, angry that they were excluded. But this time, the anger was so venomous, so deep, and so persistent that I could not ignore it or pretend that it was not significant. And it was clearly mine—it wasn't one of the little ones, it wasn't one of the grown-ups, it wasn't any of my teenage friends. It was enough for everyone, but it belonged to me.

Trust and Denial

It was seething and hateful and scary. My heart felt like stone and I know my face looked the same. I surprised myself by finally telling Susie on Friday night that my anger was not at her but had to do with therapy, and she thanked me for letting her know. I was so much angrier at you than her that it really threw me. And it made me wonder about where my anger at her really comes from because it too feels bigger than I can understand at times. I don't think I need to revisit what triggered my rage. And it will never be totally logical anyway, even though I would like it to be.

You may have noticed that I like to keep things organized and that I don't like loose ends. It can be dangerous to have loose ends.

On the subject of dangerous—I do believe that we are all still in danger. I'm not exactly sure how or why but I do feel it all of the time. When I say that my brain feels altered, it feels like I can see what is real and what is logical but it doesn't matter. What I see and what I feel were split and shattered back then—they trained me not to believe what I saw and not to feel what I felt, so it seems that those connections were ruptured. And early on, the splitting happened before I had the language to label anything, so even what I experienced preverbally was then denied or negated. Teaching me to negate my reality continued until they were gone, and then continued without them, for the rest of my life. Even now, denier lives in me and believes with all his might that nothing ever happened. period. So I live in both places and that reinforces that my brain is simply wired that way. And part of that wiring is also that they or some or one of them will always be with me, near me, around me, following me, in me.

So meanwhile, I was able to feel terrified the other day with you and to identify it as such. I can see why I don't want to go there too often. If they don't kill me, I will kill myself. Not sure how or why but I will. That message is in there loud and clear.

I think it is no accident that I cannot think anymore right now. There is more I wanted to write but I have shut down and feel all of a sudden tired.

I will try to write more if I can. I hope it helps.

And I hope all is ok with you. And with Jessie [Yael's teenage son, to whom Tommy always felt connected].

The end of this email, where Tommy writes about killing himself, demonstrates that programming was used when I was small. Many times, Yael could not understand why my memories were so tenacious, and why I had to keep going back to them repeatedly. My insistence that the Watkinses would always be able to get to me was planted in my young brain and reinforced by their daughter's letter. Thoughts of suicide were also programmed, along with dates when I would be abused again or called back to the cult.

Although my head was always filled with the noise of my (now) thirty-one alters, I heard different voices from time to time. Those were the voices of my abusers, which gradually became more and more distinguishable.

Trust and Denial

EMAIL TO YAEL

you are never going to make it (man's voice)
   kill yourself kill yourself kill yourself (men chanting)
   you won't be around anyway (my voice)
   ominous chanting, can't make out words, makes me feel like I will die.

That's all I can remember. They're gone now.

EMAIL FROM YAEL

Which part are they talking to?

EMAIL FROM SK

good question.
   initial thought would be Tommy. but also a grown-up.
   it was loud and persistent. really rattled me. I had to keep working
so I couldn't really tune in.

Tommy stayed angry for many months. He was angry at the Watkinses, angry at Yael, angry that he had to be in therapy, angry about his job which was to manage and take care of the little ones in the gang. This was the first time in four years of working with Yael that any part had sustained such negative and hostile energy.

Yael, in the meantime, was unflappable. She withstood all kinds of assaults from Tommy, and some from Raven and even Fuckface. She was dealing with more and more alters needing her undivided attention and was also once again wondering whether all of the abreacting, which did continue, was necessary for my healing. She sought guidance from various sources over the years and met once with Dr. Shelly Itzkowitz, a psychologist with expertise in DID and a large number of dissociated patients, to affirm the nature of our work. Although most of the parts were happy about the meeting and were curious about what was discussed, Tommy had quite a different reaction. He wrote this about Yael to himself, but then sent it to her a day later.

Email from Tommy to Yael

this sucks. i am not writing to her again. she is right about one thing though itzkowitz had to remind her about the trust issue. and the denial. it's gonna take time. lots of time. more time than i want to give it. more time than i have. don't have much time left anyway. what is the point really. wish i didn't always go here after anger but i do. or maybe it's really hurt. feel like an interesting study. a good case. fuck them. fuck all of them. perched there figuring us out. i can get more from those who have been through it. at least they don't come up with impossible methods of healing. talk to each other. really? bring out the parts one by one and see what they want. but don't abreact. don't go back. don't be in the memory. what do they think it is like calling for pizza. disgusts me. all of it. i was better off before. I would have been better off dead. they should all leave me alone. I will figure it out. i don't need some hot babe therapist taking me through this. and does she really want to know what i'm feeling thinking. i don't think so. i edit for her and always have. always will. can't talk anymore. it's too painful. too alone. abandoned again and i didn't see it coming. stupid fucking me asshole. shouldn't have let your guard down. shouldn't have trusted her.

Trust and Denial

I was getting closer to "whole" but there was still more (and new) work to do, which caused a shift in direction, revealing long-buried and crucial memories.

III

chapter 29

Unblending

———

Blending is when your parts take over and your center is swallowed up and unrecognizable; unblending is when your center is well-defined and you can feel and see your individual parts. Yael had taught me to unblend and put all my little ones in a safe place—on a beautiful, protected beach.

She wanted me to learn about self-energy healing practices and other kinds of parts work, but my whole system ruptured. When she asked me to find my "self," I had to move away Denier, and then Butch/Romeo (who still wanted to seduce Yael), and then mom, whose critical part got peeled away but whose nurturing part stayed behind. And on and on and on. For a long time, "self" felt buried deeper than I could ever swim, higher than I could climb. There was abundant noise for so long from all my parts who wanted to be heard; it took much more discipline than having a memory to sort through the layers of my mind and I resisted. After all, for better or for worse, I had functioned as a blended person for a long time, and change was not easy. But slowly I began to feel the benefits of not being overrun by my alters, and I was able to understand their individual functions more as I shed each one. For most people, this work involves asking your angry part, or your anxious part, or your denying part, to step aside so that you can feel your deepest emotion. These outer layers protect you from your innermost vulnerabilities. It is a system that we all can use to understand ourselves better.

This approach is called the Internal Family Systems (IFS) method of psychotherapy. It was developed by Richard Schwartz, PhD, in the 1980s. "IFS is based on an integrative model. The approach combines established elements from different schools of psychology, such as the multiplicity of the mind and systems thinking, and posits that each sub-personality or part possesses its own characteristics and perceptions."[4]

So once again, Yael and I changed directions slightly, with some tumult, but with an improved me. However, during this shift I interrupted my parts treatment with my worst memory to date, and that involved my mother. I saw her in a hooded robe, and she looked drugged. She came up to me while I was naked and tied down but then walked away with Jack. That was it. When I was describing this to Yael, she gasped. It was a gasp I will never forget, because in that moment I knew she believed my mother was involved. Jack and his group had planted thoughts in my mind that my mother did not want me anymore, that she had given me to them, and that I was getting the punishment I deserved. These things were said to me repeatedly and this was likely the trauma that cultivated my DID.

---

4 GoodTherapy.org Types of Therapy, 2018. Internal Family Systems (IFS) [online]. Available at: https://www.goodtherapy.org/learn-about-therapy/types/internal-family-systems-therapy. Accessed July 19, 2020.

The next many months after this remembering were a mixture of anger and despair. Yael's and my plan at this point was to communicate with all my parts and to have them communicate with each other. The final goal was for me, Shelley, to take over Yael's job of comforting and caring for all of them. This took another four years of grueling work that was different from the earlier years of abreacting and remembering. It is hard to completely explain what I was doing in therapy during this time except to say that I was feeling the full sadness of what happened to me and the sorrow about what it took to repair my soul.

Shortly after Tommy's outpouring of rage, which launched this whole shift in our work, I wrote to Yael:

not really sure how much longer I can do this. this is a grown-up talking. there are no voices telling me to kill myself. no teenagers being dramatic or trying to get your attention. no little ones because they don't even think about it. this is despair and it is not held by one part. it may be the exponential result of all of the despair, but it is not held by a fragment. I don't think you should keep trying to save me. it's too painful for me to keep coming back to this place after all these years. I want out. and I want you to let me go.

EMAIL FROM YAEL

I get it. You have suffered too much for too long. You want to end the suffering and when you feel this much despair, again, after all these years of fighting it and working so hard to heal, you feel completely hopeless.

Unblending

As much as it breaks my heart to see you still have to struggle so hard for some relief that doesn't feel so fleeting, I cannot and will not give up and stop fighting this fight. I love you too much to even consider that. I will hold the hope for the both of us when you can't. Don't give up on me. Please.

Email to Yael

Started my first suicide note to you. It was short because it terrified me and made me so sad that I couldn't write anymore. maybe I should write a few others.

You said that you would hold the hope, but we never talked about how you would give it to me.

This is the note:

I have thought about writing this note so so many times. How could I ensure that you are not left feeling that you have failed me? and why bother telling you how despairing I had become since you were already quite aware of that.

I think you also know how deeply I loved you, admired and respected you, and how much I wanted to live for you. I had thought that we would grow old together in some variation of our relationship, that we would weather a few more storms, hopefully share of lot of joy together as well.

But the length of time I have been suffering and the depth of my despair has become too much for me. None of the things that should give me joy are registering. There is a thick sadness that is always around me and though it lifts at times, it returns with a vengeance almost as reliably as the sun rises.

Everyone talks about the selfishness of suicide. I don't think anyone contemplating it can disagree. It is absolutely selfish. Maybe not as short-sighted as those who argue against it, since there is no guarantee that things will be brighter. Certainly not the only option, or even the last resort, since one could say that wading through the thick muck of sadness is the last resort.

Before I could write the even harder note to Susie, I had a session with Yael during which I realized suicide was not a real option for me. Because of Yael and Susie and, of course, my daughters, I held it together, but the thought of my birthday coming sent me into a new state of panic and despair. I knew that I always hated my birthday, but I had never known why. Yael and Susie both tried hard to make it a fun day, but my resistance was intense. As soon as my birthday passed, I felt better. I knew now from experience that this must have been a day that something happened to me.

In general, I was exhausted with the process of getting well. Even though most of the abreacting was done, there were still new memories and still more collisions. I was disheartened with the different types of therapy that were not working fast enough for me.

EMAIL FROM JOEY TO YAEL

dear yael,

it is me joey. i am sorry about the collision today but we had to do it and it was really nice to have you there even though i know it is pretty awful to watch and kind of awful to have too.

Unblending

i was hoping that Writer would help me but he/she has been gone a really long time and i'm not sure why. i wanted to explain what happened today but collisions are complicated and i think it is the grown-ups who want them to happen even though we always know when it is our turn to collide. they always make sense to us i guess because when they are over we feel more whole. i guess that is funny or not really to have a collision make you feel whole but it does. there is usually a lot of tension between the parts who collide until it is over. the little girl today (i don't know her name by the way) did not understand anything about what was happening but she did the most awesome thing by making Five. she has felt only pain for all these years and confusion and thinks that this happened because no one could love her and so she was given away. she also felt that when she was screaming and then when she left her body that she stayed in that cellar forever and ever. it is not a good thing that she had to make five but it was a good thing that she did. that's what she learned colliding. that she didn't really die after all. that she did something good. i think the big ones make us collide so that we are not alone and not separate parts anymore and they haven't figured out a way to bring us together cause none of us want to budge really. for me today, i needed to see where things started but more important than that i needed to feel what a little girl felt when she was being tortured because otherwise i would keep thinking that boys are better and they stay safe but really we are all in the same body after we collide. i don't think there are too many more collisions cause most of the parts have finished colliding. we didn't really expect this one but then we never do expect them before they happen.

i know that Writer would do a much better job of explaining but like I said…writer has been gone.

i will remind tommy that you are a really good mom and that he can trust you cause he is still hurting a lot and keeps getting stuck when he starts to open up or remember something new.

If you ask for me, maybe I can come out and say hi next time. I really love you a lot.
love joey

ps it would be really good if you let me know you got this but you don't have to write anything really except to joey I got it love yael.

EMAIL FROM YAEL TO JOEY
Joey –
I got it. Thanks. It helps a lot.
Love,
Yael

My parts were now flooding me with voices to attend to, and each part had a different set of needs. We were all still dependent upon Yael to help us live.

As we were trying to use IFS, Yael was wanting all my parts to communicate with one another and with my self-energy—something that eluded me for some time. What the hell was self-energy and where did it live? This was not a philosophical question but a therapeutic one. It was something I struggled to understand because there were still so many of me, and more importantly, because my whole system, which had worked for me for so long, was now ruptured; I had no idea if I even had a center anymore.

Unblending

Yael,

I guess that I need to figure out why I stopped writing. It certainly isn't for lack of material. But it may be for lack of understanding. And although I used to like to write to help me understand things better, I seem to have lost the curiosity, or I understand everything already well enough, or there is something happening which is too hard to put into words.

So since the first two are clearly not true, I need to try, in spite of the difficulty, to find the words.

I have talked about there being a shift in me, one that feels huge at times, and at other times subtle. I feel so often like I am grieving and some of what I am missing is the extreme buzz of life that I felt before my diagnosis. I miss the intensity—the highs as well as the lows—and the familiarity of my mind. I suppose that it is the strangeness of my mind, the changes in how we work together, the inability to go places where I went, that often leave me alienated from myself and lost. Every time we try something new, I have a period of such alienation that it stops me in my tracks. But our work is not the problem, and when I am not feeling alienated from the process, I do treasure us, love what we have, love what we do. I do trust you infinitely more than I should ever trust anyone, but there it is...

The loss of self is pretty dramatic, and I'm not sure I really get it. I know that there is a self there, but I'm not sure why I cannot or will not name it, feel it, describe to you who it is. I think that I am afraid that the part of me that I think is my self will end up not being real at all. It will be another part who was created by another self who I cannot identify. Everything about me and my life has been so turned upside down, I don't really trust anything I say anymore to be genuine, real or grounding. I am hopefully but tentatively waiting to discover what I thought was true is true.

I also am afraid that if I name my self and identify her, I will be expected to mobilize her to communicate with and keep track of all the parts, and more importantly, that I will not be able to lean on you anymore. Now of course, that is the point, or one of the points, of our work, but the thought of not having you to lean on, depend on, and take care of me is one step short of terrifying. Maybe not even one step short. Everything feels so huge to me all the time, and every insight or moment of truth or step forward seems to stir up the gang with so much ambivalence and conflict, it is paralyzing. This is when I go to despair—when the search for some equilibrium feels like it will never end. And it is not just the little ones who are so dependent on you. The grown-ups in me also feel like they have no idea if they are real, or constant, or really able to navigate life in a healthy way.

I don't know what the deal with Shelley is—who is she? Why don't I think of her as me? I just asked Susie about herself and her names. She was pretty clear. There is Susan and Susie and Suze and she knows who they all are. But as for me—she doesn't think of me as Shelley either. When she says my name, which she usually does not, she says it feels strange to her. So…what does that mean? I think that throughout my life, people always had pet names for me. I know that I was Shelley for a lot of years, but I have not been her for a while. Maybe when Raven stopped in time, so did Shelley. I like them both just about as much. The other problem with identifying self is that my self still includes Denier, it includes Butch/Romeo (the ultimate lover and manipulator), and it includes my mother, holder of all things critical. They are always in the room, always there when I think or write, and often there when I dissociate. Like glue, they stick to me, and it becomes impossible to tease us all apart. If you are right that the self is original and good, then obviously, I have not found her yet. I think that the difference between non-dissociative and dissociative minds is that the latter lack the confidence that comes with consciousness. If you are aware of your parts, then it is easier to see them as separate from your self and it is much easier to have them communicate with one another.

By the way, when you write [the word] Shelley, I am ok with it but when you say it, it sends a chill through me. Not a good chill.

I had planned to check in with the gang tonight while writing, since they are all usually pretty cooperative about coming out on the page. But it is late, and I am tired, and honestly, I am tired of being awake.

I may try to write more over the weekend, or I may vacate for a while.

My outer life was as busy as my inner one. I had a hysterectomy, we scattered my dad's ashes in June, and Susie had surgery for her implants. Sheer stress temporarily replaced my despair. Any stress at all tempted my parts to act out, but this was over-the-top stress and my relationship with Susie took the hit. Before my hysterectomy, I wrote to Yael.

EMAIL TO YAEL

every time I think of surgery I get a wave of shock and fear and then everything feels unreal and far away.

the first voice to appear says "why are you doing this? Why did you make the doctors think that you needed surgery?" then, I don't believe that there is anything wrong with me and think the whole thing was a plot to get attention. I am dismissive and pissy. I want to feel sorry for myself but I can't. I'm not sure who it is but I would guess that it is denier and raven and then a little of Edith (my mother), wherever she resides.

It is hard enough to anticipate all of this without adding self-doubt and criticism, but you asked everyone to weigh in and so they are doing that.

the little ones wanted to write to you earlier. they wanted to simply say to the doctors please don't hurt me. they don't want to have pain and don't want to feel vulnerable. they feel like they are back waiting, dreading, expecting the worst.

tommy is his usual boy self. he does not want to talk about it, talk about his feelings, or talk about what he might need before and after. since he needs nothing, he does not need to talk at all. he thinks that barreling through has worked before and will work again. he does not yet understand how feeling anything can be better than not feeling it. he is humiliated by the whole idea of surgery to remove a uterus, and by the possibility that anyone will assume he is vulnerable. he let all the boys know that they could play baseball during the surgery. he has not figured out what the girls can do but he does know that none of the little ones should be there.

seven is pretty pleased with the whole thing. she feels that she will finally get some attention and that it will be for something real that she can talk about. she likes that you are worried about her—she waited a lot of years to have anyone care that much who was also safe. but she is clueless about the reality of surgery, pain, and pathology. she is not really afraid of a bad outcome because it will never be as bad as what she has already lived through. she wants you to be there before during after and forever—like a mom should be, I suppose. but used to not getting much, she will be fine seeing you at some point while she is recovering.

peanut is a little freaked out since she had surgery once (her nose) and it was pretty scary. she mostly remembers how it changed her and also limited her. she was the goalie on the hockey team and couldn't play even with a helmet on. she was not too patient sitting on the sidelines. also, she was alone there before her surgery and her mom only came to pick her up the next day and kept telling her how great she looked but she didn't believe her. Alice was mad at her 'cause she didn't think she should have done any surgery at all that would change her face.

butch/romeo are not happy at all. they don't want anyone messing with their vagina or possibly their orgasms. they don't want scars on what used to be a flat stomach with an almost six-pack. they are mostly nervous about how they will feel after.

not sure who else to check in with, but too tired to do it now.

Email from Yael

Glad you were able to check in to see both how you feel about the up-

coming surgery and how some of you want to handle it when the time comes (like Tommy playing baseball with some of the boys). We will continue to devote time this week to address everyone's concerns, and plans for the big day. I will make myself available both before and after so that no one should feel alone at any time. Peanut doesn't remember Edith being by her side during her surgery—I know I shouldn't be surprised but am nevertheless horrified. That is messed up BIG TIME. Despicable.

You all are not alone anymore, and if I could physically be in the operating room holding your hand, I gladly would. Maybe you can pull a few strings…otherwise I will be watching over all of you in spirit. I promise.

The surgery went smoothly. I had thirteen fibroids removed and everything was benign. Contrary to Seven's fantasy, I did not really enjoy the attention and certainly did not enjoy the pain after. However, I did like the IV painkiller.

The surgery and a family trip to Cape Cod to scatter ashes definitely distracted me from my depression, but as I healed, I was bothered by the noises in my head. I say "noises" because while they were not always intelligible, my parts were definitely speaking to me. This resulted in feelings of conflict and ambivalence, just when I was desperately trying to figure out how I could recover more quickly. The timing of Susie's surgery and her need to be taken care of did not make anything easier.

EMAIL TO YAEL

got home cooked dinner ate dinner cleaned the kitchen bathed the kids averted a meltdown amazingly well did not get angry read a book and put them to sleep.

now I've plummeted. deeply. darkly. this is familiar. feels like [when I was] 20 [years old] when night came and all I could do was wonder why I was so despairing. not much helped though I fantasized that falling in love would. the loneliness was so profound that my body would echo from the emptiness. and now I'm exhausted. I feel like a pre-K teacher who had a class for 15 straight hours and managed to maintain control for all 15.

Excluding my time with you, it is constantly noisy with no relief. there are interruptions, conversations, visual intrusions, and arguments. and no, this has not been my mind consistently, but it has been lately.

I keep feeling like there must be something that I am wanting and not getting since I feel so desperate and hungry at these times. I'd best figure it out because there really isn't anything outside that will cure my soul and yet I can't seem to find it inside.

I assume that raven usually averts much of my despair and he isn't doing much of anything now except feeling wounded. he doesn't feel that once vulnerable, he can never really return to full rage, which leaves us all feeling a tad unprotected. I don't think we (you and I) have yet figured out how to put some things back together before I leave you, but truthfully, I am clueless as to how to do it. sometimes it feels so cruel to open stuff up and not "finish" it, not because it may be hard to look at, but because the system is so shaken that some of the simplest tasks then feel totally overwhelming.

oh this sucks, plain and simple. I guess it is progress that some of me knows that this is a moment and it will pass. but as those moments extend to days or weeks, the ability to see my way out is lost.

We sat across the table from each other at our favorite neighborhood Japanese restaurant. Susie was quieter than usual. I made small talk about office stuff to fill the gaps but nothing could have prepared me for what followed. "So, Jane's coming in on Tuesday to meet with the partners and me so that'll be nice…." Susie slammed her glass down on the table and spoke in a voice loud enough for diners at nearby tables to hear. "I've had it, Shelley. I have fucking had it. All of it. Do you hear me? Does anyone in there hear me? I can't take this anymore. You want to be with Jane? Go. I don't give a shit. I'm done. I will not let you hurt me or our kids anymore."

I was horrified. The dam had broken and she told me everything I had said and done. Years of anger and pain poured out. The more she spoke, the less I was able to recognize what, and who, she was describing. It was like she was talking about another person and, in a way, she was. Swept away in a flood of disbelief, I listened in silence for what felt like hours, and then the tears came, with apologies that, at least in this moment, could not begin to make up for her pain. "I didn't mean it. I'm sorry, I'm so sorry. It wasn't me, it wasn't me. I could never…I love you."

We left the restaurant, spent in every possible way. But it was clear to Susie that I was telling the truth and that I sincerely didn't remember. She acknowledged that I was getting better, at least better enough to hear her out. We walked to the car and drove home.

EMAIL TO YAEL

there is no easy place to begin this. Suze recounted for me at dinner

Unblending

last night some of the things that I said to her during the Jane period and while she was at her sickest from chemo. I almost wish I could spare you the details. it made Tara's Bryce [a reference to one of the alters of a character in United States of Tara, a television series about a woman with DID] look bland. afterward I told her how sorry I was and cried for hours. I don't know exactly who was crying—maybe all of us. sobbing, we told her that we couldn't believe what happened to us, while she assured us that it had. she told us that we had not been protected, that neither of our parents was there for us and that Edith participated. joey told her about the killing. He was maybe crying the most and told her that he should have died instead. he told her it was not ok to cry. raven told her it was not ok to be vulnerable. seven told her about being raped and not ever really feeling safe again. everyone let her hold us while we wept and I'd like to say it was cathartic but as I write now and am still crying five hours later I am not sure how much is still left inside. a lot I think. all of us wept for the loss of time and life. only denier was hushed. I warned her that my pattern is to feel suicidal after these revelations and this one was devastating. I was hoping that by telling her maybe it wouldn't happen but already I can feel the despair settling in. I told her that somehow we would figure out a way to keep her in the loop and keep you in the loop about what is happening at home. I'm sure this will be a hard promise to keep and will piss me off but you have to promise me that I will keep it. I don't really understand why she is still here and I am not just beating myself up. Some of the things I said were beyond beyond and the word cruel doesn't even fully describe them. Evidently I had many conversations with Jane within earshot or directly in front of her. I said things like:

Susie was bald and ugly and I was waiting for her to die so Jane and I could be together. I said something like this around Valentine's Day as well. I talked about wishing she would die and how much I could not stand to be around her on multiple occasions. She recounted her own conversations with Jane who was busy charming Susie as well, and telling her how little I knew about cancer and how Susie needed to listen to her advice and not mine. She urged her to not consult with me about her care.

She told me that one night she was in terrible physical pain and on the couch with Gracie sobbing. she said I came out in the middle of the night and saw her and laughed. then I said "crybaby. look at you, you are disgusting."

I don't think you need to hear any more. I don't think I can bear to write it and in fact, am starting to forget some of the things that she told me already.

I asked her if she could tell the difference between our normal marital shit and when I am dissociated. she said absolutely yes that my face, my voice, my everything changes. that I am mean and critical in an entirely different way.

Yael, I have to do better. I don't know how much harder I can work but this is turning me inside out. I know all that is good in that I can hear and feel all of this now. but I also know that I will still go in and out and won't know it. And that the reality of what happened to me has hit me in a whole new way.

that's it. I'm done for now.

please don't ever leave me.

Unblending

Email from Yael

I can imagine how sad you feel and how horrifying it must be to hear those words come from your mouth, but at the same time I am so glad that the gang opened up to Susie as a result. This is tremendous, tremendous progress, and probably would not have happened had Susie not shared that information with you. And I think the sharing would not have happened if you weren't in a better place—Susie could have told you before this point in time and didn't.

I hope you are feeling a little less sad in realizing that the gang is learning to trust in Susie, someone who loves them deeply and devotedly.

It's a huge step forward—doesn't mean there won't be reactions, but we will address them.

I will not leave you and it doesn't look like Susie will either.

Lots of love and hugs. It's all good. Really.

Unfortunately, more stories about Jane crashed into my world. She had called Susie repeatedly and told her that I was falling in love with her and that we had been kissing in the parking lot. Now you will ask that since I did not remember half the things I was saying, how could I remember whether I kissed her or not? I was always on guard when I was with Jane because I sensed that she was untruthful. Her mind mesmerized me in the beginning, but I was also physically turned off. I will go on record as believing sincerely that nothing physical ever happened between us. Period. Yael heard all of this and wanted to report Jane to the AMA. She also believed that nothing physical had ever happened, because she spoke with Butch/Romeo directly, and they denied having any sexual contact with her. None of the gang could corroborate Jane's story.

If despair can soar, then mine did, along with my anger, frustration, and shame about my DID and recovery. Nothing seemed to be going right and I was trying so hard. It felt like I was swimming upstream and the current was too powerful. I did not doubt Yael or the therapy that we were doing; it was more like I didn't feel I could survive it. My parts were all acting out, and it felt like everyone was screaming at me at the same time. That resulted in ongoing ambivalence, as warring forces played out their parts. Hate and Raven were in the forefront and needed to do some work in sessions rather than act out in life.

EMAIL TO YAEL

you should know better than to stir up Hate. there are different rules for Hate. it doesn't come out to talk and then retreat. it rumbles and pushes and circulates through one's blood until it overwhelms and then it comes out again. the need for protection will never be over and the disdain for vulnerability will never dissipate. and if the system is ready to die, it will help. pain does not feel good or empowering or even survivable. but Hate does. it does exactly what it is supposed to do. it drives people away and it gets you out of feeling stuck. it is action. after a while, you don't even have to think of any pain at all. anyway, whatever it does, it is still there waiting and it's not waiting to talk either.

From the little ones:
this is way too scary for us. we do not want to be in the same body as Hate.

    it feels too much like them. [my abusers]

Unblending

why do you bring parts out and expect them to cooperate? Hate can destroy everything we have worked so hard to get. and when we feel it rumbling around we can't stop it. you should have kept it in your office.

from tommy (remember me?):
I have no control over Hate. period.

from seven:
I like Hate. it saved my life in the bathroom when Jack was banging my head and pushing his penis down my throat. I would have died otherwise and they deserve to be hated as much as possible. I wanted to kill him and bite his thing off and then I wanted to drive a knife through his heart and it would have been great if I could have done that but at least I got to think about it. and I would have cut out virginia's tongue too like they cut out that little girl's tongue so that she couldn't ever talk. and virginia would never be able to lick again.

from four:
was way way too scary. they told me to put it away and so I did. or tried to. why are you reminding me?

From Shelley:
are you out of your fucking mind? this is my nemesis. this is why I can't ever own me. now what are you going to do?

Email from Yael
Firstly, I want to thank all the parts for sharing their reactions to

Hate. It's understandable that there are going to be reactions—there always are when a new part comes out. But, like everyone else in the gang, Hate had a job to do and kept the gang alive. We ALL have mean, even cruel, parts. I think the degree of cruelty is proportionate to the cruelty inflicted upon us—it's human nature and it's a survival technique. I think Hate deserves to be known and understood as much as anyone else in the gang.

Shelley, Hate seems like your nemesis because Hate takes over now in ways that hurt you and your family. We have more work to do.

EMAIL TO YAEL

thanks for writing. despair has taken over. seems that it trumps hate. tomorrow is August 5 and Lili and Ruthie will be 8 years old and I am trying supremely hard to be here but honestly, I'm not.

In this state of despair and anger and a lot of noise, all my parts got together and created a book of birthday wishes for Yael's fiftieth. It was 2011 and I had been in therapy for four years. Each part had their own page and it was as therapeutic as it was beautiful. They each wrote from the heart—their only directions were that they had to share a wish for Yael, and not write about themselves. Each picked their own font; the order of the pages was organic but overseen by Writer, who started on the first page. Shelley was last and everyone else was in between. It was the first time that all my alters had cooperated and worked together in a healthy way, doing a good thing. It was healing, and of course it was well-received. Its contents will remain private.

For the rest of 2011, I went from panic to despair to anger to suicidal and back to panic again. My sessions were intense and painful, and I re-mained desperately dependent upon Yael.

Since Lili was now eight, her explosions were more difficult for Susie and me to contain. Ruthie, the object of much of Lili's aggression, went deeper and deeper inside, and spent hours alone reading. We were all in therapy individually and together, but only a little progress was made. We were advised to create a safe space for Lili to be in when she was dysreg-ulated, and so we built a calm-down room—four walls and a rug with a chalkboard on one wall and stuffed animals everywhere. The room was tiny, and Lili hated it, but it was the only place where she and we could be safe. Putting Lili into a room and locking the door triggered me every time, and my anger at her was often out of control. This would have been enough for me to deal with, but unfortunately there was more.

Before Susie and I were together, I raised two stepchildren with Mau-reen, my first and only other long-term partner. My stepson JT was eight when I first met him. In 2011, he was forty-two and was my dream son. He is kind and generous and intuitive. He lives in Boston with his wife, Danielle, a special woman who fast became the family favorite. My step-daughter, Peggy, was five when I first met her. She had a troubled life. She was obese and bipolar and had borderline personality disorder. By 2011, at the age of thirty-nine, she was married, an alcoholic, and addicted to prescription medications. She had been furious with me because I would not give her money for fertility treatments and had become increasingly abusive over a period of two to three years. She started calling the house and screaming at me and threatening me, Susie, and the girls. It was ag-onizing but I had no choice but to get a restraining order because I was afraid of what she might do. In January 2012, Peggy died of an accidental overdose of alcohol and drugs. Her husband felt I was partially responsible and was enraged with me. Fortunately, Maureen and JT did not share his feelings and were incredibly supportive. The three of us had a unique perspective, having known Peggy for a lifetime. It has taken years for me to come to terms with her death and to feel the full sadness of her life—another in a series of heartbreaking memories of a difficult time.

chapter 30

Some Parts Recycled

I thought that once parts came out and had their memories, I could move on. Yael and I were both surprised by their tenacity and their need to return to the room repeatedly to process and unburden their pain. Each recycling was a bit different, and although their growth was apparent, it was still exasperating and depressing to never feel fully finished. The power of their pain always took me by surprise, in part because Denier had been working, and in part because I had been so hopeful that the entire process would not last for as long as it had.

Little Girl had been the first alter to come out and tell her story with all the terror and panic that she felt but was unable to express at the time of the abusive event itself. Even five years after her first emergence, she was still scared. She was not used to writing but she saw all the others doing it and wanted to try. Some of the others checked in as well.

Some Parts Recycled

FROM LITTLE GIRL TO YAEL

Its rainy and cold and dark and i can't help thinkin aobut all thos nites wen I wondrd whre they we taking me exsep i relly new alredy and I hopd that someone insid me wuld hlp me but I wasn't alwys sure they cud and somemtiies i feel that way wen i'm with you that im not relly sur someome will come out and help me then and if I new for sure then I mite be able to tell you more aobut what happnd or at lest it woldnt feel so scary.

Mabe you can tell the big ones not to leve me.

FROM TOMMY TO YAEL

I have a bad feeling that something is coming up but I don't feel like it's a good time for that to happen.

Shelley really wants it all out. everything. she believes that anything left inside will be toxic. and that it will hurt her at another time.

I don't think that any of us feel that we can really heal completely. how can we really?

Anyway, I'm thinking about exercising or skating or something just a little bit more. I didn't forget. Every time I see your nails I feel like a jerk cause I didn't hold up my end of the bargain. but I will. good thing we didn't put an expiration date on the deal.

I am keeping the gang moving right now. Slowing down will make it hard to manage everything that we have to do.

Miss you by the way.

FROM DENIER TO YAEL

The gang read me an old letter of our dad's last night—it was about the importance of drive and ambition. It's hard to explain why but it really rocked my foundation.

not that I'm wanting to be challenged but I am into the truth.

so I'll bring you the letter tomorrow. nothing about the abuse in there. but he was so fucked up. their marriage really makes sense now.

I'm glad that you understand why I need to hang around. I think that you already know that I know what happened and that my job now is to manage when and how stuff comes out.
everyone does miss the old me though.

EMAIL FROM BUTCH/ROMEO TO YAEL

We took a break and it was pretty nice. The gang liked it anyway. But we're back!! Can't really talk about the abuse too long without stirring us up. And we do still need to do some work with you and better to do it in the winter when you have more clothes on.

EMAIL FROM YAEL

Hi Guys –

Some Parts Recycled

Thank you for writing. I would love to check in with each of you tomorrow (if you are up for it) so that we can talk about your emails. Love you all.

EMAIL TO YAEL

trying not to sink which really means trying to stay busy. five has decided to hang around and wait to see you next week if he can. david doesn't want to write for him. tommy is pissed about something and butch/romeo went back into hiding. they don't like being out when it is cold. little girl is scared that five is back out and so is seven. shelley is overwhelmed with life and her parts and her pain and tommy's anger. and raven's. it is floating at the surface, right above five. peanut is stirring but needs butch/romeo to be out for some reason. everyone wants out and no one is volunteering to go first.

I hate my DID—it still shocks and surprises me and wears me down. I need to write but never have the time.

now I am going out to a movie but I don't really want to be anywhere except under the covers.
    I'm also tired of bitching so I'll stop.

love,
the gang

EMAIL FROM YAEL
Hi to the gang —

I think we have to find a way for more of you to be working in the room. Everyone needs something individually, but I also think that you are capable of learning to work together. I know that may sound presumptuous on my part because I DON'T understand the energy and effort it takes to navigate your internal world. But I think we can find a way to make it easier to communicate and understand each other. What do you guys think?

Email to Yael

From your lips…
trying to get Lili into a timeout today while she was fighting me and she twisted out of my arms and smashed her head on the door frame. I wanted to pack and leave. This is horrible for me, for the little ones, for the whole gang. there is little peace inside.
Love you.

––––––––––

The nature of Yael's and my work was changing and as it did, I was miserable, resistant, and gloomy. It was time for me to start helping all the parts communicate with one another and also time for me to take over Yael's job as primary caretaker of the gang. I wasn't having any part of it and sank back into a deep and dark state of mind. Yael, who had always been sensitive to what was good for me and necessary for the process, began to assert a change that I found uncomfortable and plain awkward.

Before, the work had felt more organic—I came into sessions and started talking, crying, remembering, or abreacting. Sometimes I shot the shit for as long as I could get away with it. It was not that I wasn't working hard but it did not require profound intellect or a lot of discipline. It did not make me feel like I needed to go against the stream, so to speak. But we had entered a new phase of work now—one that was crucial to my integration but more perverse and difficult in a whole new way.

I was not good in session today—or, I should say, I felt horrible. too depressed and agitated to object to anything directly, but negative and dissociated anyway.

no matter how I feel when I come in tomorrow, I am telling you now that I am sinking into another hole that is dark and hopeless. this is exhausting. I don't even know how to do what you are asking me to do in session. I feel brain dead and paralyzed when you ask me to check in. I miss you. all of my parts miss you…but that is not helping them to come out. They have certain patterns that they are used to and are reluctant to share time with Shelley even though she is feeling open to most of them. even B/R has her sympathy right now.

I feel like I have gotten the one-two punch—first this summer seeing my DID and grieving and now realizing how I have abused Lili. the reality of how my present life has been affected by my abuse and has affected those I love is too much to bear.

It is like no matter how much work we do, I am still seriously dysfunctional and seriously suicidal. there is still so much shame that I am pushing you away. and when you don't back off, then I think that you have lost your perspective.

I'm a mess.

Tommy was still struggling with being a multiple—he didn't understand how he could "see" Joey and Five and David and all the others and they could all really be him and thus me. And how could I take care of them if they weren't real? The whole thing was hard to figure. He also felt, having watched Shelley and the rest of the gang, that he had his own denier and he was hard pressed to accept the imminent sadness that he knew would come from believing the abuse really occurred.

EMAIL TO YAEL

Yael,

I cannot complete a thought in my head without noise, but here is what I know.

Tommy wants to revisit the rape at 7. He wants to make some emotional connection that he is missing.

He also wants to know when he split and created raven, hate and fuckface.

No one is feeling connected to the abuse right now. It is like that horrible period of grief after facing yet another recounting of my dissociated comments has been turned off and put away, and that denial has moved back in. it didn't occur to me that once gone, it would return, but it has. or it has for tommy. I'm really not sure.

I think we need you to take us back, or be more directive, or more confrontational, or something. asking me to check in, or to bring parts into the room, is not working without a context. I'm not sure if my agitation is a part not wanting to come out, or me not knowing how to get them to come out. I feel tremendous pressure lately to work with my parts but I don't really feel them a lot of the time. and when I'm shut down, it feels impossible. anyway, I'm way too tired to make any sense of all this now, but I do know that I'm needing something and not getting it. so there's something to noodle on. this process is definitely not a linear one, and sadly, it feels like sometimes I need to double back to pick up some momentum.

Gradually, that's what Yael and I did together.

chapter 31

Safety Plan

By the time the girls were nine years old, they were both in weekly therapy. Lili was continuing to have dysregulated behavior and Ruthie was still the object of much of Lili's anger. Lili's tantrums were now more explosive and difficult to deal with because she was older and bigger. My reactions to her behavior were equally out of control. I (Raven) screamed at her and held her roughly; occasionally I slapped her or pushed her away with force. Susie seldom left the house because she wanted to protect Lili. I was furiously trying to deal with the parts of me that were reacting, but I was triggered constantly. Lili's therapist, Clare, felt that her mandate was to protect Lili and she worked with us to come up with a scrupulous plan:

- I needed to see a psychiatrist, Dr. Lauralyn Fredrickson, to see if my reactivity could be controlled with medications.

- All of our therapists needed to speak and consult with one another on a more regular basis.

Safety Plan

- I was not to be alone with Lili until Susie felt it was safe.

- Susie and I needed to see Dr. Elizabeth Howell, a couples therapist who was also a leading expert in DID.

So Susie and I went back into therapy together, and this time around, she was angry with me, really angry. She was angry about my rage and my loss of control at home. She was angry about my abuse of her and the kids. She had many reasons to be angry and they all came out. Our new therapist, Elizabeth, had written an important book about DID and was part of the DID clinical community. She knew exactly how to talk about my parts and validated Susie's feelings. Elizabeth was soft-spoken and gentle, but she did the job.

This entire experience was seriously sobering for me. It was a wake-up call like no other. I was ashamed and saddened and felt overwhelmed with the responsibility to change my behavior (to get my parts in line). It was time for Yael and me to take another look at the way we were working. And we did.

Although Raven and his gang had been there early on, they came out dramatically after several years of work with Yael. It was the aftermath of this emotional upheaval that forced me to release Raven's gang into consciousness. This is when I could finally feel the rage that was building up over the course of my unconscious and conscious life. These alters were each identified with my abusers, and so they were extremely hateful and evil. It took me a long time to recognize that they were protecting me, and it took me even longer to be willing to communicate with them. I was afraid of them coming into the room because they thought of hurting Yael. Hate did not have a voice, but Raven did and Fuckface was exactly what you imagine—vocal and unbelievably cruel and murderous. These alters were deliberately created by my abusers to make me more like them and could take part in the abuse of others. As an adult, these parts were the most destructive to my relationships because they not only existed, but were dissociated; I was not conscious of them. If told about my behavior after the fact, I could not even make contact with the reality of what was being described to me.

Having these alters come out in the room so that they could be re-associated or integrated was of utmost urgency. Although they rarely came out at work, they were repeatedly out at home and with my kids. These are the parts that scared my family the most, and the parts that shamed me most profoundly after their appearance. Unlike normal relational anger, which everyone experiences and often expresses, my rage was extreme and frightening. Susie did the best she could to intervene with the girls, but the hate that was directed at her was difficult to deflect, even as she understood where it was coming from and why.

Clare's intervention and safety plan while this was happening forced me into greater consciousness; probably because my rage and shame had become public.

chapter 32

Boundaries

————

Anyone who has suffered abuse struggles with boundaries. They are either without any, or they are so walled off that they cannot be intimate or in any real relationship whatsoever. I was the former—I had few boundaries and in fact, didn't even understand what boundaries were or what they were good for. As far as I was concerned, what was mine was yours and vice versa. For years, I gave patients personal information if they asked, and in my youth, felt that anyone who wanted to go to bed with me could do so. I did not have any sense of what was legitimate privacy and what wasn't.

My previous therapist, Carol, not only missed my diagnosis of DID, but toward the end of our work together, lost her sense of boundaries with me. I met her family, hired her nephew's girlfriend to work in my office, and gave her menopause advice and a prescription for hormones. She even saw me in my office, although we were at least clear that I should not examine her. It is unfortunately common for patients with a history of abuse to be abused further by their therapists. Some become sexual, which is the most destructive thing that can jeopardize a therapeutic relationship. Had Carol asked for a medical examination, I would have given it to her. I had been conditioned for obedience and my job was to do whatever was asked of me. Period.

In the end, I was lucky that it ended with Carol when it did.

It was now 2012 and I had been in therapy with Yael for five years. She and I talked about boundaries incessantly. I was always pushing for less rigid boundaries, and she pushed back. Our work, however, was intense and a certain closeness was inevitable given the amount of nurturing I needed. Her job was to keep me safe and to somehow communicate love for all my hurting parts. My job was to accept her love as nonsexual, which was a near-impossible feat for me, and to not take advantage of the closeness that we had. After all, I texted and wrote to her on a regular basis. I knew where she lived and all her phone numbers. I knew things about her life because we spent six to eight hours together each week for years. Yael did not have as strict boundaries with me as some therapists might have, but I never felt that any of our interactions—either conversational or physical—were inappropriate. She got terrible headaches and I wanted to cure her but that never happened. One time, she was in so much pain that I wanted to send her home. I also tried to give her medication that might help. Our boundaries got blurred and Yael pulled back. It was the first and only time that our relationship was challenged. Yael was also trying hard to stick with the IFS therapy and not slide back into memories and abreactions. The gang reacted extremely poorly.

EMAIL FROM THE PARTS AND SHELLEY TO YAEL

From the little ones:

we hope that you don't get mad at us and go away and we are also sorry that we need to know so much about how you are feeling but we need to know that you will be ok and always there

From Tommy:

I was telling shelley and the gang that they were getting into trouble with trying to take care of you but they got really pissed at me for interfering and then I got pissed at Susie cause she wants to take care of everyone but that's my job and it makes me feel totally inadequate when she takes over.

From Doc:

not me this time. I wanted you to take care of yourself and tried to get you to the right doctor so that I could stay out of the room.

From Mom:

guilty as charged. I totally wanted to take care of you and my boundaries are pretty blurred. I see your pain and your vulnerability as much as I see your strength and your wisdom. I love you unconditionally which some-times gets me confused and I do the wrong thing. Selfishly, I also wanted you to feel better so that you could help me with the little ones again.

From Tommy:

There is really no point in my coming back to see you. The pain is un-bearable and because I lived through it once, it doesn't mean I need to do it again. If I'd known how painful getting "well" would be, I never

*would have started. I don't think you get it. why would you abandon
me if you knew it could kill us?*

From Shelley:
*this was one of the worst weekends ever. I feel like I completely lost out
to tommy and every angry part of him and me that exists.*

*the good news is that it did not spill over onto my family. but that
is probably because I was either shut down or in my room crying.*

*I feel totally alienated from you—waiting for a rescue that did
not and is not going to happen, and still feeling furious that I allowed
myself to trust you and be dependent on you. whatever the reality is
regarding how much of a shift was needed in our relationship, I have
gone to the worst possible places one could go.*

*It is no surprise that my wounds feel disproportionate to what re-
ality would dictate, and that for me to feel alone, abandoned, unim-
portant, and pretty much discarded by you is a first. I have yet to figure
out how to let you know when I seriously need you to check in. short of
holding a bottle of pills or standing on the ledge, nothing else seems to
warrant a call for help. and it seems that you agree.*

*at any rate, I am here and technically alive. I still feel like I don't
want to see you. maybe some time will give me perspective. maybe it
will make things worse. I don't know.*

*I have a terrible week ahead with lots that I don't want to deal
with. right now I am holding on.*

EMAIL FROM YAEL
Hi Tommy—

I am responding to both your emails.

I am in no way abandoning any part of you. I think we are both going through a transitional phase in our work together. I am confident that once we reach the other side, we both will have grown from the experience. Getting through it is the hard part. I can't and won't "make you" talk this through with me. I also know that I can't want you to get better more than you want to get better. That never works. I remain committed to helping you and the gang.

Email to Yael

You should be reaching out to me. I am a mess. Or maybe that's against the rules. you need to be fucking ok now because I'm not. Every morsel of every bit of abuse is in these tears. I can't work. I can't think. I don't know what is safe and what isn't.

Email from Yael

I hear how much pain you are in and how angry you are at me. I have been responsive to all your emails and have not been operating under any new "rules." I remain committed to working this through with you. I am not abandoning or discarding you in any way. I do, however, think it would be best to sort this out in person with you tomorrow. I am really really sorry if I am doing something to make you feel these painful feelings—it is not my intent, ever.

Boundaries are fluid, personal, and not always clear-cut. Every good therapist sets boundaries that are comfortable for them, given the client and the nature of the work. Yael and I worked intensely, spending many

Boundaries

hours a week together. I needed to be re-parented and I needed modeling of normal healthy behavior. Re-parenting was essential to my recovery, and for me, required some physical nurturing.

My little ones needed to be held at times or have a hand to hold. Some of my older parts needed a hug as they were sobbing with grief. Physical contact had to be okay for both of us, and it was. Today, Yael and I always hug each other goodbye because it has been a long, arduous, and heartfelt journey, filled with mutual respect and love.

chapter **33**

Integration Is Not the End

Over the next year, my parts became more integrated. I had not finished dissociating, but I could remember
when I did, and I did not need to travel to such great lengths to
get away from my pain. I did, however, still have pain.

EMAIL TO YAEL

Dear Yael,

*I wish I could write but Writer is nowhere to be found.
It feels like a lot of unblending has happened and a lot
of grief has come along with it. I'm not sure you get how
many relationships were going on independently and how
the parts are still there but they're not and I feel better at
times and then something happens to stress me out and
then the parts get all messed up but they don't have their
own private time with you anymore and it feels like 27
people [the number of my then-known alters] have broken
up or lost their mom and I get that I'm supposed to pick up*

from there but the grief is overwhelming and it isn't over yet. Each one of them feels the presence of the others and they know that they are no longer so separate, and they also feel like they have instantly acquired twenty-six brothers and sisters to share everything and everyone with and they don't feel all too happy about that. Add to that the collective grief as they ALL start to feel what each of them held alone and the pain is screaming. This is probably why so many multiples have argued against integration. It is yet one more excruciating thing to do before feeling better and it has no inherent appeal.

I'm going to sleep and hope that tomorrow is a little lighter. It is mind-boggling how much work there is yet to do…that alone makes me cry.

EMAIL FROM YAEL

To the gang –

Thanks for writing—it's really helpful to me. I can see that you are in a tremendous amount of pain, but I obviously have no idea what is going on inside. Sounds incredibly complicated and painful beyond measure. It's so unfair that the healing process is so long and harrowing. You are a survivor in the truest sense of the word, and I know that you are determined to get better—and you WILL. I am with you all the way.

Much love,

Yael

With integration came an ability for my parts to communicate with one another. I could access them doing this although I was not in control of it. This is in complete opposition to the way things were before, when each alter operated independently and switched to another without any awareness on my part. I was often surprised at the relationships between parts that were developing yet overwhelmed by the realization that I would ultimately need to be in charge. The whole system was changing and concurrently I was feeling everyone's panic and grief. It was no longer compartmentalized and unconscious.

EMAIL FROM TOMMY TO YAEL

Dear Yael,

Tommy here. Seven is attached at the hip and she wants me to join her somewhere. When you asked me today how I felt about Shelley, the question kind of hung in the air. part of me was shocked that you asked it, part of me shocked that it was a reasonable question, part of me is still shocked by the whole system. but to answer you, I think mostly that I feel sad for her. make no mistake, she is the one ultimately calling the shots, but I do know that she doesn't feel like she has any control over the gang half the time. and harder than feeling sad for her is feeling sad for me which is seemingly even more frightening than feeling my anger. I feel kind of beaten down. I have no passion, no spark, no nothing. I am kind of sexless and ageless and completely depersonalized. I am not fighting the body I am in because I don't feel embodied at all. I think I am still trying to figure out if they killed me. or killed my spirit. I know I've been functioning but that really doesn't mean anything about the life I am living. and I used to feel more playful, especially with you, but that's gone. it almost feels like I grew up all of a sudden, and I have no idea how to handle adulthood...real adulthood.

Integration Is Not the End

> *I will try to pick this up tomorrow. I must try to get some sleep.*
> *love tommy*

There was still some fallout from our meeting with Clare. The gang felt that only their angry parts were acknowledged, and that the rest of us didn't exist. They hated the intrusion by other professionals. It was now the summer of 2012 and I wrote to Yael:

EMAIL TO YAEL

I do not believe (nor do you) that every moment with Lili was potentially a dangerous one. I do feel that within a short time, you and I could have and would have identified safe times and unsafe times. I was willing to not be with Lili alone at all while we worked on this. However, I needed to feel like I was participating in those decisions and not being seen as someone who was out of control, even while acknowledging that this part of me has been out of control. But once parts are recognized, if nothing else, their power diminishes, since they are no longer free to function autonomously at any time. They are not rendered powerless or inactive, but once they are recognized, understanding what triggers them comes quickly. I may have felt that no time with Lili was safe for a while. I would have liked to weigh in. But instead, I was ordered by the team and then left in limbo to await what??

Does anyone know us better than you and I? Is a psychiatric consult necessary for making a plan, or simply to complete the team so that everyone's ass is covered? Do you really believe that Lamictal or anything else would have prevented this part from emerging? And acting out. I am not arguing against seeing someone, I am arguing against their having an opinion that is worth anything more than yours. I am happy that you will have support, and I will be happy if medication helps me to feel better. But it doesn't mean much more to me than that.

Anyway, my anger and my pain are pooled together into a giant black hole. All of my shame has overloaded and overwhelmed me, and my little ones. All the work we did feels temporarily (I assume) undone and nonexistent.

And although most of my adults recognize the need to protect Lili, there are still little ones who see her as the abuser and who feel completely alone and forgotten. Shelley is doing her best to take care of her little ones, as well as Lili and Ruthie. She is at war with Susie for all the reasons you know. And it was not the best time for you to question my dependence on you. I don't think anyone angsts over my dependence more than I do or yearns to be free of my neediness. To hear your concern about it made me feel even more inadequate at a time when I was already submerged.

I was desperately struggling for control and felt I was losing the battle. Lili's safety was the priority, but my little ones could not understand why their fear of abuse from Lili was not just as important. I did not feel anyone could understand this as well as Yael. I was outnumbered, and rightfully so. Lili's safety *was* the priority and her therapist *was* right to demand what she did.

Discussing this with Flannery turned out to be eye-opening and heartbreaking. All of this had triggered her own memories of growing up with me, and although Flannery was not a child who needed any physical restraint, she certainly experienced her share of my frightening and verbally abusive behavior. She questioned whether she would have memories of physical or sexual abuse, but fortunately, to this day, she has not. I have no recollection whatsoever of any abusive behavior toward her. The possibility horrifies me beyond words.

Now that my parts were co-conscious, I needed to work on the things that might and could continue to trigger me to dissociate. My hateful and evil alters were still tormenting me and I was determined to contain them, if not extinguish their behavior completely. Yael always told me that I could not kill off any parts, but I could give them new jobs to do to protect me. I still wanted to banish Fuckface, Raven, and Hate, along with **Junior** (the name given to the alter who was my abuser, Jack, living inside me), but they were there to stay, testing my mental health at all times.

EMAIL TO YAEL

I've been particularly cranky and irritable at home. I don't usually come out other places because I don't need to. The gang has plenty of good reasons to be irritable without my help—they are working really hard, physically, spiritually and psychically. They haven't been sleeping much at all. They stay up until 12:30 or 1:00 and then don't really sleep well and then get up at 5:30 or 6 to be ready for the onslaught of children, cranky and irritable themselves. The whole Lili fiasco had them reeling, still does, and they haven't even begun to process and accept what is coming from Flannery. Doc, speedy and mom were fine not seeing you today. Doc in particular had so much work to do that the extra few hours were put to good use. The rest of us, me included, had a rough afternoon and were really disappointed, and then became unglued. Even Ruthie got us going, though it was Lili who pulled me out and kept me out. That was until tommy and mom had to pull Susie off Lili because she looked like she was going to kill her dead right then and there.

I first noticed how present I was when I was home with Ruthie alone. Kids don't come much easier than her, but she does get spaced out and moves slowly and it drives me insane. I want to throttle her into motion, and I become mean and hateful, waiting for her to come out of her fog in the shower and wash herself. She's so happy just standing under the water, and when I've come in for the 4th time and she still hasn't done anything, I want to make her feel shitty. And I frequently do. She has to understand that if she doesn't keep moving, she will be in danger. And also, she is too spaced out to see anything coming, which fuels my rage. If she doesn't move things along, then I can't stay in motion, and that makes me panicked and claustrophobic and furious. And that was just Ruthie. Then there is Lili in the shower. She is singing and dancing and chattering and spraying water and having solo conversations at break-speed pace, and it is her freneticism that drives me to the brink. That and the fact that I am talking to her and she doesn't hear a word I'm saying so after 3 or 4 attempts to speak in a normal voice, I scream. Then she wants to know why I am so mean and screaming at her. I warned Susie that I wasn't going to be able to stay with her much longer, and indeed, I left after another minute of her hyper-ness. You and I know about chaos, frenetic noise, and things moving too fast. Tonight I felt so crazed and had to work so hard not to blow, that I might have cried. A tear or two. As soon as Susie started screaming and grabbing at Lili and saying that she had had enough, some of the gang stepped in cool as could be. I watched and was really relieved that I was no longer needed. I started to feel

*calmer, or the gang did, at any rate, and was able to hold onto Lili
(not all that tight either) until our calm passed through us and into
her. Then she was fine. Then I was fine.*

*But now, they are asleep, and I feel miserable. I feel isolated and
shamed and I'm afraid that I have way more grief to get through than
I ever thought could exist in one person. I feel like a monster. Not quite
as monstrous as Jerry Sandusky, but not a whole lot better. I guess that
I am assuming that Flannery will remember something sexual, that
my denial will hold me for a while, and then I will crumble in shock
and pain. I think the only reason I have not crumbled yet is that I can
see that Flannery has survived, and I am not so certain that Lili will.*

———

*took a break. Fuckface is gone now. watched parenthood. cried some.
played my bass. heard from Flan who is hurting so much.*

*I'm thinking that I should call Fredrickson [my psychiatrist], or
maybe write to her. I don't think the Abilify is doing anything but the
dose could be wrong or the drug could be wrong. then again, I haven't
killed myself yet. there is no question that this evil part has become
unhinged. I still hate calling him junior and there aren't any names
that are evil enough in their own right except for Jack and I will not
name a part of me Jack. so I am thinking of other names—ones that
are toxic or poisonous—ones that can take another person's soul away.*

*I hope that you are feeling a little better. please let me know. I'm
sorry if that feels intrusive. I'm sorry that you are hurting. and I am
really sorry that I can't heal you. god that pisses me off. it feels like that
could have been a good karmic trade for us. for me to be able to give
back—not that we need to feel any more bonded than we already do.*

also, tell me again the dates you are going to Mayo for your head-aches.

we are all sending you much love—and hope that it makes it through the pain and even disrupts it a bit.

see you Friday, I hope.

much love,

Shelley and the gang and writer and Mister Unthinkable and Out of Control Fuckface (I'll work on shortening it)

Email from Yael

dear MUOCFF and the rest of the gang —

thank you for writing. Especially about the kids' behaviors that trigger you so, and for telling me now how some of the others are doing.

I hope we can get to speak a bit tomorrow.

I too was disappointed that I had to go home yesterday, but I'm taking some new meds that lessen my pain, so I am not planning on missing any more work.

date of Mayo starts on Tuesday 11/27/12.

see you soon.

I know you are fighting hard to hold it together, and in my opin-ion, you are doing an amazing job. AMAZING. Trust me on that, because I know you may not recognize that.

hope the gang has a better night's sleep.

love always

Now that I was almost "whole," I did not understand why my reactions still seemed to be so severe and extreme. I fluctuated between good and bad, joy and misery, and panic and boredom. I was furious with Susie for reasons I can barely remember, except one. She was not writing screenplays or earning any money and the burden of supporting the family was killing me. One night, Susie's sister phoned and I vented as I walked along the Hudson River. She was sympathetic and agreed that Susie's not working was messed up and unfair.

The next day, Susie got a frantic call from her sister, who told her that I was crazy and she should leave me ASAP. It was a terribly upsetting call for Susie but her defense of me helped us turn a corner. I felt sideswiped and betrayed, but our joint anger was good for the relationship.

Halloween was approaching and still had a dark power over me. I was certain that there was cult activity on this day when I was young, and I always grew panicky at the beginning of October.

This year was no different and the likelihood of my dissociating was high. To add to my stress, on October 30, Hurricane Sandy hit. We were left without power or water, and as I sat in the dark with candles burning, I thought that this could be a potent distraction from Halloween. Tommy rallied, getting into survival mode, and was his usual macho self. He wanted to take care of everyone and make it all be an adventure. Unbeknownst to me, Fuckface was right at the surface, and he emerged for a horrendous interaction with Susie. She had gone out to walk our dog after the wind had begun to pick up but before the rain started.

Sometime after she left, she buzzed to come upstairs, and I assumed that she had forgotten her keys. I told Ruthie to buzz her in and open the door for her. When she walked into the apartment, I knew she was hurt, upset, frightened, or all the above, and I could see that her jeans were wet. I knew that the hurricane was unfolding and accelerating but I myself had not been outside. What happened next was a switch that caught me completely by surprise.

What I felt was *Oh now what?*

What I evidently said and the way I reacted was far worse.

After having her repeat twice, as she entered, "Shelley, I'm hurt, I need you here," I begrudgingly got up, saying, "Jesus, you can't even walk the dog without something happening." In fact, she had been clipped by a flying piece of plywood, 8 x 4 feet in size, probably traveling ten to twenty miles per hour, continuing its flight for two blocks, and causing a cab to swerve out of the way. She'd been struck above her ankles and she was already swollen, cut, and bruised. And I was already annoyed and disdainful. I felt she was being too loud and I told her to quiet down so as not to frighten the kids. I mustered enough sympathy and presence to clean her wound and bandage it properly (the only part of this incident that I enjoyed) and then nagged her for the remainder of the day about being on her leg too much, not resting, not taking care. I was sweet a few times and asked her if she needed anything, but I was faking it—and I knew it.

Often, I look back at things that I have said and realize that probably most people have felt some of these ways at some point in their relationships. But they have filters and don't say everything that comes into their heads, and they also don't lose the moment in consciousness. I was unfiltered and unconscious, and Susie was the primary recipient of my venom. I know my disdain for her vulnerability originated in my abuse; I have always felt that showing pain was tantamount to death. The little girl in my past whom I helped to kill was crying out in pain while they were screaming at her and then killing her. Was this a real memory, was it staged? I will never know, but to me as a small child, it was real and its repercussions rippled into my life for a long time.

———————

By the end of 2012, I was starting to have more light days than dark ones, and was feeling slightly more independent of Yael. We were successfully using IFS in our sessions. Yael would ask certain parts to come out, or to get out of the way of other parts, so that each part was heard. It felt a little weird to me, but the few times I was able to consciously bring parts into the room and hear them, the healing was profound. Getting rid of my pain involved unburdening it. For me, that often involved imagining my abusers as victims of my rage and hurt. For each terrifying scene in my young life, I could do whatever I wanted to do to Jack or Virginia or any of the cult. For example, Seven wired Jack and electrocuted him until he was no longer. After engaging that image, the memory no longer held the same power over me—it was neutralized.

The IFS process can be complex, especially in a multiple, but because of it I was able to get much better, so much so that even my skeptical self tells me that it worked.

EMAIL TO YAEL

it has been so long since I've written. so long since I could parse the voices inside my head. maybe even so long since anyone had much to say.

I realize that during times of change, the gang has always cooperated and gone along with Shelley. She has insisted, I suppose, that life would be virtually impossible to navigate unless she could make certain movements without unanimous agreement. Not all of those changes and decisions were the best ones, but then whose are?

so these past few months have qualified as change in a big way. the past few years really, but we've covered a lot of that already.

speaking of covering, my IT guy Daniel was able to restore everything to my phone since my last hard sync, which was end of November, so all of my texts and photos are back. I was thrilled and a little overwhelmed. I think I won't be transcribing any more texts, unless there is something spectacularly important. another change.

so back to the last few months. as horrible as my dinner with Suze was where I discovered how brutally dissociative I was, that did not hold a candle to hearing about my abusive behavior with my kids. My limited alone time with Lili and Flannery's distance from me are both daily reminders that fuckface and some of the other charmers have been out and about recently.

I know I still have a lot of work to do, and in some ways, it has gotten much harder to do the work with you when all of the other parts have unblended. I have to yield to your suggestion that it is time for parts work, since my symptoms are no longer driving me to revelations. It all feels so much more contrived, and for lack of better terms, so conscious. It is different, that's for sure. But I get it, and maybe I'm ok with the changes in our schedule because I do get it. If my symptoms aren't driving me, and I know I have to unburden myself, it makes sense that I should be not only ok, but kind of happy to cut back sessions. I think I am too old to confuse my love for you and my dependence on you. The former will not change but the latter is neither pleasant nor desirable. Even getting my texts back made it clear to me that 1) I don't need to keep reading and rereading our texts, and 2) we are never going to get that book written!!

Ha!!

chapter 34

My Mother and the World of Denial

By 2013, I was largely integrated, which by no means meant that I was finished healing. My parts were identified, and they were talking with me and with one another. Fuckface and Raven were more contained, although not completely inactive. I had many better days, but the bad ones left me in a dark place that could see none of the good. It was as if I'd never left the basement.

Yael was moving her office from the building I worked in to further uptown and I had no idea how I would handle the change. I had been going to her office for six years for many hours a week. Familiarity and trust were integral pieces of our work together and I was on edge.

Bigger than these things was that I was having flashes of my mother's involvement. Most everyone in my life who knew what happened to me and who knew my mother agreed that she had to be complicit in some way.

My Mother and the World of Denial

EMAIL TO YAEL

… So I guess there are lots of good reasons for why I feel all stirred up and then my mother called at 4:30 in the morning to ask why I never call.

I hope that this all means that parts just need some attention and not that more stuff is coming up. I know that we will deal no matter what, but I would like to feel that some things are finished, that some parts of this process are over.

As I check in, I can tell you that the little ones are ready to talk. They are jealous of and angry at Lili and Ruthie for monopolizing my time. Tommy has been waiting patiently to deal with a few things (his own DID in part, and some physical/sexual things). B/R feel like they finally showed up but are not done and still feel like I want to get rid of them (this is only partly true). Peanut and seven are just so sad and I imagine this has to do with Edith, who just doesn't deserve to be called mother. The little ones are probably sad too, but they don't feel sad, they feel needy, which is probably the baby version of depressed.

EMAIL FROM YAEL

I am glad to see that you are checking in with your parts and that they are telling you what they need. I will make sure that these parts are attended to in therapy.

And she did, but not without a certain amount of resistance.

EMAIL TO YAEL

resistance

> *always one of the worst parts of therapy.*

funny since I know that is what it is and what it is about, and I shouldn't be surprised and therefore not resistant but I am.

and I know what you would say.

you don't have to go back there.

why don't we ask inside and see if anyone wants to say something?

like that makes it easier.

of course they don't want to say anything.

no one wants to commit. no one wants to utter the truth. and no one wants to feel its full impact.

no one wants to really say they believe it.

because it changes everything...it casts a whole new shade of black on my life, my perceptions, my memories, especially the good ones.

it really was bad enough to ingest the truth of the horrible and de-humanizing abuse. but that does not hold a candle to seeing my own mother participating.

in any way. actively or passively, though actively does feel far worse. even more incomprehensible than her just letting it all happen.

because she loved me at the same time or at least gave me that mirage to see. but she loved herself more. that's really it. she was always more important than we were. than anyone was. she took care of herself first and we were left helplessly behind.

and what if I'd been killed? would she have twisted that into her own suffering narcissistic crisis? Lots of attention for her then.

do I really want to know, need to know? will it really free me or just weigh me down more. how happy will I ever be knowing that my mother abandoned and tortured me. what satisfaction is there, really? what liberation, if any?

how many antidepressants does it take to lift a beaten soul?

I am tired, Yael. I look for deep reasons for my fatigue, my yawning, my nodding off. but I am tired. I can't get this off my back and now, I need to really process being in a new office, at new times, with a tectonic shift in my weekly rhythm.

maybe this will shake me up and shake the system down to the bottom of the well. and maybe truth lies there, deep down, waiting for me.

I hope so. my heart is so heavy I feel it sinking into the abyss. it hovers over a black hole, fighting gravity, only a baby step away from plunging downward.

and my soul feels broken.

you will need to work some miracles. but first you will need to settle, and I will need to wait until you're ready.

Memories of my mother moved in and out for many months to come. And Denier was right there to greet her. I was as incredulous as Yael when I arrived in session telling her that nothing in fact had happened to me at all, ever. I could never come up with an alternate explanation for why I suffered from DID, which at this point I accepted. But Denier didn't seem to care much if I could explain things or not. Recognizing that denial was a critical defense for my survival helped me some. The fact that my denial could come and go over the course of fifty minutes also convinced me over time that shit happened. Really.

EMAIL TO YAEL

Today was pretty miserable. I felt the same as when I was having mem-

ories all the time and was just trying to get through the days. I have this sick feeling all the time. I can't eat, I'm having nightmares and terrors and I'm exhausted. I should just spit out the Edith memories and get this misery over with, but my parts are not cooperating. They have their own rhythm and timing and logic, and I am at their mercy. I know that I'm supposed to be communicating with them in a more reasonable manner, but the denial is so powerful that I get blocked at every turn.

I'm not even sure who holds the memories of Edith's involvement, since in truth it should be held by all of the little ones and by tommy and writer and raven and mostly everyone except maybe the grown-ups who came later in life. And in some twisted strange way, I really want to discover that she was there—it feels like it would be a relief. And it does feel like the last giant hurdle. So if I want to see her in a memory, and I haven't, then what does that mean?

Denial?

I can see Edith's angry eyes—and her coldness and ability to completely lock everyone out of existence.

I didn't see it often, but when I did see it, it was pretty chilling. I saw her ice out my father many times and she was never apologetic when her cold period was over. She just assumed that we would all be there waiting for her, which in fact, we were.

I hate her so much that I feel sick thinking about it. But that would be true, or is true, because of everything I have already remembered about her. Her handing me off seems to be enough to earn my disgust, but why, why, why do I keep looking for her in the rituals? How crazy could she really be?

Even I, dissociated as I am, did not subject my kids to cult abuse.

My Mother and the World of Denial

I did abuse them and not know it but going over to the dark side for any period of time requires a whole other level of dissociation.

I really think that she saw a lot more than I've remembered, all at Jack's hands, and all horrible. But probably not down in the basement or the place of rituals. Probably in the house, in his house, at the "doctor," at our house, in the car.

While in Cape Cod that summer, Flannery and Susie engaged in an animated discussion about my mother's cruelty. I just didn't see it, although they had many a story that corroborated their beliefs. I spoke with my brother shortly after this discussion and he had no problem believing what they had said. He told me that when my mother discussed my past with him, she asked, "If all that was happening to her, why didn't you stop it?" He was incredulous and said, "Mom, I was five!" She never brought it up to him again.

Over the years, both Susie and I had discussions with Edith that were damning. Things that she had denied originally came to light. She said at first that Jack was strange to her and she didn't like him. Then it turned out that they were "very close," although she never admitted having an affair with him even though she had confessed to having relationships with other men.

Then, in later years, Edith said Jack used to babysit for me when she ran errands and that he had a "capacity for covering things up." By the time she was in her nineties, she told me she wished she had taken better care of my brother and me. She also said that she did not feel connected to anything or to herself in the past. She acknowledged having no real memory of when Bob and I were young.

My Mother and the World of Denial

She described her life as someone else's. We have since concluded that my mother was likely dissociated herself to some degree, and that she may have been abused as a child. Jack had far more access to me than he should have. In session, I remembered him abusing me in front of my mother. I also remembered Edith having sex with Jack. I was small, probably three years old or so, and was not supposed to see what was happening. I, of course, did not know what sex was at that age, but I was able to describe some of what was happening in my memory. I later deduced what was going on as they were in bed together and I saw them kissing.

In 2013, I recognized that some new memories were coming up and that they were about my mother. I had already had a memory of being taken to the "doctor" by Jack and my mother and left with the doctor alone. I was four years old and I was called **Four**. I was sexually abused by him, and told that I was being punished. I am uncertain what my mother knew but I am certain she left me there alone. With this recollection I began to have more panic attacks and my despair reappeared.

Then I had a memory of Edith penetrating me anally. This was not a ritual and she was not with Jack.

EMAIL TO YAEL

there is a cry deep down inside me that is unlike anything I have felt before. everyone has asked, including me, what difference it would make if she were involved or not. and I never really had an answer. now I do. I would liken it to having my heart cut out but that does not do it justice. there is a bond, a primitive bond, between mother and child, which is now broken, shattered and irreparable. there is screaming pain that starts in my gut and explodes through me.

*the moment she touched me in my memory was the moment every-
thing changed. I was still ok up to that point, rationalizing and understanding how misguided and how pathetic she was. I could think
that she was drugged or coerced or held hostage, but I could not imagine her violating me, not in a million years. my heart is broken now.*

I need some time before I can check in with the gang, but I will.

I love you much and wish you were here.

EMAIL FROM YAEL

*Thought about you all weekend. My heart hurts for you. I don't know
what else to say except that it will get better. It doesn't get worse than
this. I want the gang to know that they are amazing and brave and
that telling you what they remember, however horrific, is the only way
for the gang to heal. I continue to be in awe of all your parts—and
what they had to do to survive.*

Sending you love.

Although this made everything make more sense, it was devastating
to remember. Denier's questions about how these abusers had so much
access to me, where my parents were, how this could have happened in
my own house, and why it went on for so long were all suddenly clarified
and answered by my mother's complicity and involvement. My father was
essentially out of the picture; he was working constantly and relegated *all*
parenting decisions to my mother.

Years earlier, before I had memories of Edith's involvement, I had asked
my dad: "What did you think of Jack?"

"I didn't like him much. I didn't trust him."

My Mother and the World of Denial

"Why not?"

"I helped to get him a job and he screwed me out of all the money I was supposed to get. I just didn't like him."

My dad was no longer alive when I finally believed my mother was a participant in my abuse, and I doubt that I would have told him anyway. As I write this, my mother is a few weeks shy of ninety-four and has dementia. She does not recognize me and has no idea what is going on minute to minute. My brother and I, for reasons that we can only surmise have to do with our own moral compasses, have taken extremely good care of her as she has aged. I suppose that I have forgiven her, although seeing her can still agitate the gang. There will never be resolution or satisfaction, and I will never get a firm confirmation from her.

Fortunately, I have not needed that to heal. This does not mean Denier is silent. I still exist somewhere between the world of belief and the world of denial. Perhaps I always will. If someone with knowledge about my past approached me with confirmation, I would probably come apart at the seams.

EMAIL TO YAEL

things haven't been so good at home, according to Suze.

I've been critical and a little nasty with her and I have been forgetting a lot of things that we have talked about.

she of course, STILL, did not email me when I said these things and so I asked her, yet again, to please email me the conversations when they occur.

I don't really think she gets DID.

I'm depressed, for a change.

Shame and grief, shame and grief, non-fucking stop.

My Mother and the World of Denial

EMAIL FROM YAEL

I am not surprised that you are struggling at home. That doesn't mean that you should expect to be aware of it when it happens. You are right in assuming that you are acting ok unless told otherwise. I know how upsetting and discouraging it is to hear that your experience doesn't match Susie's perception. The reality is you are feeling multiple feelings at any given moment—how can you possibly know? A lot of change is happening in your system, but that doesn't mean it feels encouraging— or like there is an end in sight. I am sorry that it's still so painful for you. I just ask that you try to be kind to yourself. Please. Sending lots of love.

Giving credit where credit is due, Susie and I tried just about everything. We were now in couples therapy once a week with Elizabeth and we each had our own individual therapists whom we occasionally saw together. We also had both of the kids in therapy and had meetings with their therapists regularly. Plus, we had our psychiatrists, along with Lili's, with whom we met every few months.

At one point we had ten therapists and psychiatrists for the family. The expense was enormous, and we were feeling financial pressure. We remortgaged the apartment to get through the next few years. And yet, there was still more work to do...there was always more work to do. Susie found it next to impossible to write, much less to travel to Los Angeles to pitch. Emails to and from her agent became less frequent. She felt isolated from her career and guilty that she was unable to contribute financially, all of which left me feeling constantly angry.

My Mother and the World of Denial

I was pretty shocked at how far away I went during our session with Susie on Tuesday. As soon as she started talking, I became young. Seven and younger. You were the grown-ups and I was to remain quiet. Obviously, I was not prepared to deal with my dissociating during the session. At one point you asked me how I was doing, and I felt caught in the headlights. Today we saw Joe [Susie's therapist] and I did much better. We talked a lot about old patterns in our relationship, what we would both like more of, how to recapture the good that we'd always had. Several times, Joe must have thought I was wandering off and asked me. But most of me was pretty present. He asked what it sounded like in my head, and I think Susie was pretty surprised by my answer. (Do I need to describe that here?)

As much as I went away on Tuesday, I think I heard most of what everyone was saying. I will compare notes with you, I suppose, and find out if that's true.

I don't know who is writing this email.

But just one day later, I wrote this:

EMAIL TO YAEL

...I HATED having Susie join my session. I felt childlike and inadequate and I was angry that you let her talk so much. It felt like you could have had the session without me sitting there and maybe should have. And that this surprises you (which I think it does) worries me

about how well I hide things. And what was I hiding? Bottom line is that it is not good for me to be talked about for any stretch of time, and it seemed like you let her go on for the whole session.

I understand that this may not really be the way it went down, but it is the way I experienced it.

So I guess I'm pissed at both of you for talking about me like I wasn't there. Or feeling like you did. whatever. My session with Joe at least included me more, which is maybe why I reacted better.

EMAIL FROM YAEL

Hi Everyone –

I am so sorry that it has been such a supremely hard week. We have a lot to talk about and work through including your reaction to the session with Susie. I'll just say this—I shouldn't have underestimated how triggering it might be to have her come and be a "threesome" again. Historically these sessions ranged from barely tolerable to unbearable for you. I should have done a lot more checking in about it with you and for that I am really sorry.

Much to talk about—good thing we have three sessions this week. Please don't stress about that either. No timetable. no rush.

The best that I can figure is that: 1) I was possessive of my relationship with Yael; 2) I was used to dissociating completely with Yael and felt quite free to do so, whereas I tried hard not to dissociate when I was aware of it, with Susie; 3) Susie was and is a talker who can go on at great length about things big and small, and I think I just plain resented her taking up my time in session; and 4) most of what Susie was doing in our sessions together was talking about my dissociative behavior, which in her experience was mostly horrific.

The rest of 2013 was erratic. I was putting little pieces of the puzzle of my life together and was still unhappy at times with Susie as was she with me. Was this normal marital shit or all the detritus of DID? Who knows? The kids were not easy...at all. I had cut back my sessions with Yael and was missing the time with her. I was writing less, which was probably a good sign, but it also left me with more stuff to work out in the flesh. Despite or perhaps because of all this, I was getting better. Work became much more enjoyable for me again. My partners and I had finished a huge renovation of the office (which I directed, my dear friend Donald designed, and my brother built) and it turned out beautifully. It was clear that as my survival occupied me less and less, I needed to seriously deal with my ongoing dissociations at home.

Susie and I continued working with Elizabeth, which was invaluable during this period. Despite Fuckface still being persistently around, we were successfully negotiating our stuff, and I was slowly but surely becoming kinder. Susie was less depressed, thanks in part to her own pharmacologic help, and we were working better as a team with the kids. We'd been told enough times that we needed to model kind and loving behavior, and we were determined to accomplish this. At the end of 2013 and the beginning of 2014, I began writing this book. Susie was enormously helpful and encouraging, especially when I needed to stop and put it away, which I did for months at a time.

We had plenty to improve upon, but most of the nastiness was gone and Fuckface was relatively quiet. I didn't think of sending Susie off for tests or doctor's visits without being with her. I didn't let her go to Trader Joe's alone anymore and carry all the bags, which was difficult for her because of her neuropathy. She was in pain all the time, but I no longer minded that she was vulnerable and that she expressed it. There were times when Fuckface was with me and saying nasty things in my head, but I'm pretty certain that I was not repeating what he said. Susie had been—and still is—my rock through all of this.

There was still a tremendous amount of pain and despair in my life, but it didn't last for as long as it had, and it was countered by many more happy moments. I still did not understand why, once my memories had been exorcised, I did not feel immediately better. My mind was certainly quieter, although I could still access individual voices.

My parts were being cooperative…most of the time. But as it turned out, there were still more memories.

Email to Yael

waves of panic. All the little ones are popping out like moles.

writer is on sabbatical and that doesn't help things at all.

I can't seem to get a handle on this but it feels really old and like we've been there before but I don't want to be there again and sometimes the panic is just a part popping up and sometimes it is a memory which is like a part I guess but more complicated.

I can't possibly be having any new memories and I see no logical reason to revisit the old. so what the fuck?

my cough is nonstop again so I started a steroid inhaler and will try to talk less which helps.

I know I am running on and on a bit but I'm hoping that I run out of anxiousness even if I don't figure out why I am anxious. Like who cares really anyway?

speaking of caring, I think that my motherless life is just starting to hit me. I can be a little slow at times. but when all the abuse is teased away, horrific as it was, the realization that I was not mothered is so overwhelmingly sad to me that I start to wonder how and why I survived. and no wonder I miss you so much lately, especially since cutting back.

a few of the little ones want to speak:

From little girl:
i know it's over but sometimes it just feels like it's going on now and I don't really understand why that is happening. it makes me feel hopeless. and disgusting. i'm not sure tommy is around to help either.

From joey:
i feel scared lately and bad. i was thinking it was all over but now i'm not sure. every now and then i pop out at work which is not a good idea cause i don't really like it there and i don't want to see naked women in fact i don't want to see any women except you. where's tommy?

From seven:
just feelin sad. there is this fear hanging over us.

From peanut:
I'm ok. But tommy doesn't seem so good.

From tommy:
I've been wanting to talk but you know it's hard for me and hard to

*even figure out what's going on. writing the book is a huge trigger for
me cause I think it's just too hard for me to listen to what happened
to the little ones again and especially now that I understand that they
were me too and all that stuff happened to me as well as them. I just
can't really believe it all sometimes and it makes me want to run away
and hide and not talk and I really don't want to take care of everyone
again cause I get lost and then there's no me left. I hope I don't have
a whole lot more work to do with you not that I don't like seeing you
and all, but it is soooooooooo hard for me. And I really can't deal with
being a multiple. it's too fucking weird.*

From doc:
*gotta get back to work. we don't have enough money to come back
Tuesdays. ☹*
xo
doc

Because I was writing this book, I needed to fill in a lot of blanks and
Susie was the main person to provide that information. She told me about
times in the beginning of our relationship when I was like another person,
and a crazy one at that. I thought of all the other people in my life along
the way whom I may have hurt inadvertently. I went back and read many
journal entries and emails that I had written over the past seven years, and
even poetry and journals from my college years. My despair and thoughts
of suicide were gripping, and the reminders of just what had happened to
me were too much to bear. The pain of the present wouldn't abate, even
though I was so much better.

My Mother and the World of Denial

During this period, I had a new memory of being held under water in Jack's bathtub. This was Little Girl's and Tommy's memory and it caused me to dissociate again. What this precipitated was another round of screaming in my sleep, and feeling angry, discouraged, and depressed all over again. I started writing about grief and all the reasons for mine.

Also during this period, I was finally able to do serious work in couples therapy, but it was difficult. Elizabeth was incredibly fair and gentle, but my relationship with Susie needed a lot of work to heal. Also, our family dynamic was seriously chaotic. We were lucky to find our way to Tim, a gifted child and adolescent psychologist at New York University, who began to turn things around for us all and especially for Lili.

It seems that our life was like a reality series, called *Couch to Couch,* about a family that spends most of its free time and all its money seeing different therapists. There were some days when Susie and I had three appointments to attend and by the end we were utterly exhausted and brain-dead. There were also many times when we felt so discouraged that we would fantasize about moving to the country where life would be calmer. Lili could have as many animals as she wanted, and Ruthie could ride her bike to school. And everything would be magically better.

During this period, I was getting to know two new parts: a **waiting** part who did not have a name, and **Eraser**, who was responsible for deleting bad events in my present life. For example, we would go to Lili's first therapist, Clare, and I would say that Lili had had a good week. Then Susie would remind me that Lili had had three meltdowns during which she attacked all of us and was verbally abusive. I would sit there dumbfounded. Of course, I was still dissociating, but I was also erasing memories as they occurred.

My Mother and the World of Denial

EMAIL TO YAEL

I am mute.

That is my reaction to today's session, and I can't seem to shake it.

I think that it brought back not only the grief, but the terror.

I still get to a place at times where I can't really believe what happened and I guess that I was there before I saw you.

My waiting part feels so overwhelming and dark—it's hard to imagine that I function when it is present.

But I think that it is almost always present, and I think that I am always a little bit depressed...or a lot of bit.

I think that is my biochemical reality.

How MUCH do you think the brain rewires? Do you think that doing parts work rewires us?

Being mute helps me to not feel the pain. It's probably not the best reaction for Susie to live with, but she seems ok with me tonight.

I will try to talk about some of this (my waiting part) tomorrow with Howell [Dr. Elizabeth Howell, our couples therapist]. We will see how that goes....

Oh well, I thought that writing would help but it didn't. I still feel like I can't really speak.

This just has to pass I suppose, in time.

I will see you Monday and by then eraser will surely have worked its magic.

But now you will know how I felt.

EMAIL FROM YAEL

Glad you were able to write. I can't imagine what waiting must feel like—like a nightmare that you never wake up from. I can only imagine the burden it's been carrying, and I suspect it's pretty huge.

I believe the brain rewires because your progress is proof of that. I believe more than ever, really, that we are built to heal, and it may take a lifetime to get there, but the payoff is there. I wholeheartedly believe that you can and will experience more joy, more presence and less pain. You are indomitable, Shelley. You really are.

Love to you and your whole remarkable gang

I always loved Yael's optimistic-bordering-on-Pollyanna emails. I realized while writing this book that she was pretty careful not to do email therapy with me. I did a tremendous amount of writing, but we never really had much dialogue via the mail. I needed to know that she was there and craved a kind or loving word or two but there was not a lot of banter. Over the years, I learned that she would not respond to my Friday missives until Sunday night, and many of my weekday emails went without a response at all. I knew that the work needed to be done in the room, but I also knew that I could never let her know about all of the things I was feeling without writing about them. It is mind-boggling to me that I wrote more than a thousand emails, and extraordinary to me that Yael was able to read them and hold my thoughts as well as she did. And she was really treating over two dozen different clients at the same time.

The entire rhythm of our sessions began to change with my needs and honestly, I did not like it. I often longed for the old ways, because they were familiar to me and because I was taken care of. Now I needed to step up, grow up, and take care of the gang, and I resisted at every turn. Yael was forever patient with me, and slowly I began to see the benefit of independence. With that came the responsibility of accessing my parts when necessary, talking to them, taking care of them, and teaching them that we were all going to be alright. My mind, at this point, was ever so much quieter, without thirty-one-plus voices vying for my attention. But dissociation was devious, and it snuck up on me still.

In 2014, Halloween was, as always, intense. I had long ago established it was a day I associated with rituals, and every Halloween in the early years was horrific for me. But the holiday had become more tolerable and so I was caught off guard when I became edgy and disconnected and then refused to go into a Halloween store with Ruthie to pick out a costume. I felt kind of "zoomed back" in time, but once the holiday itself passed, I was okay. As it turns out, this time of year is extremely difficult for Flannery as well. I'm sure this is a direct consequence of my dissociation every October as well as that her other mom, Maureen, was usually grieving for her dad who had died in November years before. It is just a shitty time for all of us.

As the year ended, we reached a point where we were starting to think about therapeutic boarding schools for Lili, whose behavior was close to unmanageable, and our hearts were breaking. She was so young to be sent away, but there were those in our circle who thought that this might be the best option for her. Ruthie was desperate for calm but not if it meant Lili living out of state. She tried to make peace with the possibility of it by researching schools online—if Lili *had* to go away, Ruthie would do her part to find the best school in the world for her sister. All of this was so hard for us, individually and as a family, to process.

One night, in a moment of fury, I reportedly told Lili that we were sending her to a wilderness program and that they were going to come "in the middle of the night and take her away." Lili, shocked and terrified, burst into tears, screaming, "You can't do this to me!" Susie, furious, took Lili into another room, held her, and promised that we would never let anyone take her away from us. I was horrified...*horrified*...when Susie recounted this to me. But I was also angry that she had, once again, neglected to write this down for me when it happened and only told me about it a few weeks later. I felt that she was not doing her part to help me be aware of and manage my behavior. She did not dispute this.

I was still dissociating with both Lili and Susie, and I knew that it was Fuckface I had to deal with. "Dealing" with him meant letting him come into sessions, recognizing his contributions to the gang, understanding where he came from, and then tempering him as much as possible. If I didn't rein him in, then he would continue to protect me in a way that was hurtful to others, and that wasn't working for any of us. Being conscious of one's parts is ninety percent of the battle and once you can see what is going on, you just need the will to change it.

Fuckface stuck around for a few more years before I subdued him, although he is not extinguished. I can still hear him rattling around and having thoughts, but the outbursts are pretty much gone. This is not to say that I don't get angry, but it is normal anger; I remember the circumstances and what I've said.

chapter 35

Almost There

_____

For the next two years, Susie and I struggled with two children in crisis and were just holding on. Ruthie had slipped into a serious depression. Lili, after all the work we had done to help her, was still having tantrums; with a great amount of hesitation, we hired an educational consultant to look for boarding schools. In the meantime, Lili was still working with Tim, and we were hoping for miracles. Ruthie was in therapy with a psychiatrist, Doug, who was whip-smart, soft-spoken, and funny. She connected with him immediately and he helped her begin her healing process. We were hemorrhaging money and pain but no one can say that we were not getting the best care there was in New York City.

Ruthie was miserable and remained so for much of middle school. As I write this, she is out of her depression, thriving, and doing excellent work at an outstanding high school—one of the most competitive in the city. She is mature and politically astute, and plays a mean guitar. She is thinking about becoming an investigative journalist. She will be great at anything she chooses to do because she is smart, compassionate, and hardworking. Her relationship with Lili has changed for the better and now they have an unbreakable bond.

Lili worked with Tim for a year and things improved to the point that we abandoned the educational consultant (who took our $5,000 deposit, having done no work other than meeting once with us) and thoughts of boarding school. When Tim felt that he had done as much as he could employing his therapeutic modality, he referred us to Dr. Francheska Perepletchikova, the world's leading expert in dialectical behavior therapy (DBT) for children. We saw her weekly for two years and she worked miracles. Lili graduated from DBT therapy in early 2019. She attends one of the best schools for very bright kids with learning differences and is thriving both academically and socially. She is bright and funny, and has a terrific group of friends. She loves animals and has done community service as a volunteer working with dogs at animal shelters since elementary school. Interested in forensic science, she has watched every episode of *CSI* and obsessively reads books about mythology and the mysteries of the ages. Her goal is to become a forensic psychologist. We have no doubt that she will accomplish anything she puts her amazing mind to.

And then there's Flannery, our incomparable Flannery. She has grown into a healthy and beautiful woman. While she still has some remembering to do, if she so chooses, she is happy now and has a full and enviable life. After graduating from NYU and the Institute of Culinary Education, she formed a private catering company with her best friend, Lauren, and is now a well-known and accomplished international chef, who doesn't cook nearly enough for us because she is too busy traveling and working. She is part of a sailing collective and travels all over the world cooking and being a first mate. Again, enviable.

Susie is now ten years past her original breast cancer diagnosis and it has been almost three years since she was found to have metastatic disease. She has had bilateral mastectomies, reconstruction, exchange of implants, removal of one implant due to sepsis, and removal of the remaining implant electively. Her implants caused her tremendous pain and kept her from sleeping comfortably for six and a half years. She had tried to do the "right thing" by having reconstruction, but she made that decision with little information about how uncomfortable the implants could be. I was no help, thinking that reconstruction was the way to go, and not having heard from patients about their own negative experiences with implants.

It did not really matter to me what decision she made. At least I thought that it didn't. But when the last implant was out, and I faced the reality that she would not even look like she had breasts, I was temporarily distraught. After all, I was a victim of the same culture warp that she and all women have been subject to. So, it took me some time to get used to the new her, but eventually I did. I think her reconstructed breasts enabled me to forget to some degree about her cancer but more recently, when she had (thankfully minor) surgeries for melanoma in situ and an excision of atypical cells in her tongue, it all came rushing back. I worry constantly about losing her. I am trying to live in the moment, trying to be more mindful and present. When her tumor markers went up recently, I lost some ground in my mindfulness and was swept into a swirl of fear of her death and our family's loss, but I try to be thankful for every moment we have together, which is a much more fulfilling way to live.

Almost There

Today Susie and I are better than good. Taking care of her is my highest priority. Fuckface rarely lingers in the background, and when he does, I certainly do not articulate what he is thinking. I will never understand why Susie stayed with me, but I know I am blessed that she has. It took years for her to forgive me and for me to forgive myself, but we are a good team today. We are taking it a day at a time, and at least I am present.

There was light at the end of this long tunnel, and I could see it for the first time ever. I could also see that life was not going to be perfect, because it never is, and that I will still have the same stress that every other New York City doctor mom with three kids married to a woman with Stage IV breast cancer has. And that is stressful indeed.

My brain has been largely soothed and my soul has been loved and renewed. I did not find God, but I found peace and mindfulness and humility. There is no longer noise in my head and I am now able to cry almost on cue, at just about everything. Yael changed my appointment day recently and I forgot to show up. That was the first appointment I missed in eleven years! I guess I was just feeling okay enough that day to forget.

I have often wondered: if you have DID, do you always have it? It is hard to imagine that it is just gone, especially as I feel so strongly connected to all my parts. And there are times when I wish I could willfully dissociate and get away from the pain, and I still can, in a small way. With healing comes presence of mind, and because I felt for so many years as if mine had been taken from me, having it return is the greatest of gifts.

Afterword

As I finished writing this book, my mother—after a year of complete dementia—left us peacefully in a lovely nursing home at the age of ninety-five. I whispered in her ear that I forgave her and that she could let go. She died the next morning. Had I given her permission? Who knows?

The person who mothered me, however, lives on.

AN OLD TEXT MESSAGE TO YAEL FROM PEANUT AND SEVEN
Do you really think this is ever going to stop hurting?

TEXT MESSAGE FROM YAEL
I do, but hurting is the only path to healing, unfortunately. It is so terribly unfair to have to suffer so, again—I want to believe (and do) that hurting in the presence of someone that can love and protect you in a way that you need and deserve is a transformative and powerful force. I'm glad that Peanut and Seven reached out. OXOX

Afterword

When I began therapy, my symptoms were unrelenting panic, suicidal depression, and drug addiction. Yael's goal was to get rid of all three. She was optimistic and ready for the task at hand. Therapists, it turns out, must be as prepared to do trauma work as the patient, for the hours are long, the degree of abuse is severe, and the pain is unthinkable. Her goal was to reach all my parts, talk to them, care for them, and allow them a voice while leaving me whole and in charge. My goal was to survive the process. Her promise was to see it through and so was mine. She was going to take care of me. And take care of me she did. Anyone who has done trauma work knows that the relationship with your therapist is intense, exclusive, and loving. There is a bond of trust which cannot be broken, or everything falls apart. Yael was as skilled as she was natural, as funny as she was sad, as serious as she was playful. She absorbed all of the rage that I could purge, and she gave me back love in its place. She kept track of every part, numbering more than thirty, and loved them all equally. And in the end—and there really is no end—she helped me to unburden a lifetime of grief and pain.

We exchanged hundreds and hundreds of texts and emails over the first six years of therapy. Our work was 24/7 or at least it seemed to be. I needed to be re-parented and Yael's commitment to my recovery was nothing short of lifesaving. Yael would text me and the gang, often with emojis of hearts and x's and o's, and Susie would see them and feel jealous. Understandably. I had little emotional energy for her or for the girls during the roughest times and our relationships suffered. In later years, I was able to return emotionally to my family and there were plenty of heart emojis for Susie and the girls.

It is hard to put into words both what happened in my sessions and how this bond grew over the years. Yael was taking care of thirty-one of us and there was only one of her to go around. Competition and jealousy were rampant, as is typical for most siblings and their parents. But there were a lot of us, and Yael had to keep track of everyone's feelings. I frequently forgot what happened in sessions or even things that I wrote or messages that I left. Yael not only remembered but had the unpleasant task of telling me about some of the awful things that I had recalled and told her. Although she may disagree, she seemed to change with each alter she was working with. Her voice, her body language, and simply the way she communicated had to change to meet each alter on their level. And sometimes I did not know I had switched until she recast her expression and directed her words to the newly present alter. This was yet one more thing that persuaded me I was indeed dissociative.

My sessions were grueling, and persistently so. I was depressed much of the time, and anxious when I was expecting new things to come up. I hated having memories, dissociating, and being panicked. I hated the way I felt before a session and afterward. At times I felt self-destructive and had to check in with Yael when I made it home. Several times I wanted to throw myself into the middle of the road, these being programmed thoughts.

Every now and then I would have a session that was calm and I would get hopeful that I was cured. Sometimes this feeling lasted for a day or two, and then I would be slammed with more memories, collisions, or abreactions. I often wound up on the floor screaming, and Yael would be right there with me. In my eyes, she was the perfect mother, protecting and comforting me when I was in distress, and teaching me by her actions about love as I had never known it. She caught me each time I tried to escape, and for her, it was exhausting and affirming at the same time.

Afterword

All my parts, but most especially the little ones, felt completely dependent on Yael for everything. They could not see, because I was not ready, that I would be there for them as Yael had been for me.

Even the concept was mind-boggling.

We developed a rhythm with one another after so many years together. I could usually read her, although in all honesty, she always seemed steady and there for me. Her sadness and sometimes disgust with my memories, however, was always evident and affirming for me, and the few times she wept when I was a little girl were powerful and healing. We are all so tied into the reactions of the people we love, but children especially need that modeling and I definitely received it.

For anyone with DID who is looking for the right therapist, it will take time to know. Trust is essential for any parts to feel comfortable coming out. If your therapist questions the validity of your memories, leave quickly. If they make you feel safe and loved, and they can skillfully deal with your different alters, then you will probably get better. If you fall in love with them, it is normal and will work itself out appropriately, as long as their boundaries are clear. I was more than lucky when I found Yael, and we both believed it was in some ways karmic that we would work together.

As I write this, I consider myself largely recovered. I continue to see Yael for a single session—a mere fifty minutes—weekly, down from six sessions a week at our peak. I rarely text or email, unless it's to tell her about a terrific book I've read or a movie that she must see. Occasionally one of the little ones wants to say hi. Occasionally the grown-up me needs to connect. We are immensely comfortable with each other and share a history that is intense and amazing. Now I have the usual ups and downs of life to deal with, and I probably still dissociate during severely stressful times. But I usually know that I've gone away temporarily and can usually catch myself and come back.

It seems strange after all of this to write about how lucky I am…but I am. I have a wife who loved and sustained me for many years, friends who were there for me, and partners and others at work who supported and tolerated my transition to health. I have three beautiful children—constant reminders of what is most important. Finally, we each had therapists who were and are extraordinary and I had one who saved my life.

I am lucky. And so happy to be alive.

Postscript

There are those who experience unspeakably horrific trauma and are forever shaped by it. And there are those who have not themselves experienced that same trauma but nonetheless find that they are deeply impacted. The pain is different for each and is felt by both. I could never have imagined, that day in the spring of 2007 when Shelley walked into my office, the deeply painful journey we would make together and the remarkable relationship that would develop between us.

I was in college when I saw the movie *Ordinary People*. Judd Hirsch's portrayal of Dr. Berger, the kind, patient, wise, and devoted therapist absorbing Timothy Hutton's anguish over not being able to save his brother from drowning, was, simply put, extraordinary. The depiction of the journey from trauma to healing through the power of the therapist/patient relationship was, in part, what drew me to become a therapist myself.

Why did I believe that I had not only the ability to relate to and understand the depth of trauma some people carry

Postscript

with them but the desire to become part of their healing process? As an Israeli American, the Holocaust was never far from my consciousness. Even as a young child, I read everything I could, asked endless questions of family and friends, and became obsessed with trying to make sense of how people survive the most unimaginable horrors. I didn't have the ability to change the reality of what happened, no one did, but maybe I could help them process memories that paralyze and, in some measure, help them heal.

When Shelley and I began our work together and she grew to trust me, she slowly revealed the extent of the physical and emotional abuse she suffered and the excruciating pain she experienced from what was, in truth, torture. It started when she was a baby and continued for seven years. As she recalled and described each of the countless times she was brutalized by a group of adults who were part of a ritualistic satanic cult led by her next-door neighbors, it was clear that an incredible thing had happened. Her young, innocent brain had created different parts of her personality to experience and hold the memories of the events so that "Shelley" didn't have to. It was as though she would leave her body the moment her abusers began one of their rituals of terror. How did I know this? That there existed different...parts? We would be in session and suddenly her voice changed—and so did her body language, mannerisms, vocabulary, handwriting, gender, age, and name when recalling a particular memory. Each part held a different experience, a different pain, and her parts became what we called "the gang." We started to meet frequently, often three times each week. We talked, texted, and emailed outside of sessions. The therapeutic approach was unorthodox, to be sure. It became clear that our work together would likely continue for years. Because in order to help Shelley heal, it was critical that each one of her parts be acknowledged and heard, and made to feel safe, accepted, and loved.

As a clinician I was, of course, familiar with DID (dissociative identity disorder) but had never met or worked with a "multiple." The graphic reality of what had happened to this innocent, defenseless child was beyond belief and often almost too much for me to bear. But as Shelley began to reveal more and more of her parts, it left me with zero doubt about making the diagnosis of DID. When I told her, it seemed that the weight of decades of not knowing, not being heard, not having a name for her symptoms, feelings, and behaviors, began to lift, if only a little. She was relieved, but now came the excruciating work it would take to help her heal and, ultimately, make peace with all of her parts.

Some would question, understandably, how the experience of being tortured to near-death and controlled by members of a satanic cult can possibly equate in any way to the devastation that six million Jews experienced at the hands of the Nazis. My answer, unambivalently, is yes, yes it does. The trauma Shelley survived was unlike anything I had heard of, much less seen, and it did, in fact, mirror much of what the Nazis did to the Jews during the Holocaust. Every survivor has a story to tell, whether it is on a grand scale and part of our history or instead small, individual, personal.

I believe that Shelley and I found each other at the right time in our lives. For me, the work we did united the two desires that formed the basis of my decision to become a therapist those many years ago. First, I wanted to explore with greater clarity the overarching questions that drove my curiosity when I was young and obsessed with understanding the Holocaust: How do people survive the most unimaginable horror? And how can that horror even exist in this world? And secondly, I wanted to look back at my

Postscript

career someday and think that, in some fashion, I was able to be someone's Dr. Berger—the caring, committed, and patient therapist who takes on a broken soul and embarks on a painful journey in service of knowing and understanding her truth.

Words fall short in my attempt to articulate my feelings for Shelley and the unique relationship we built. The imprint she has made on my soul is deep and everlasting. For that I will always be grateful. Shelley is a woman of unwavering grace and indominable spirit. Knowing her story, knowing her truth, is as great a gift as I can imagine.

Yael Sank, MSW, LCSW
July 2020

Acknowledgements

There is a lifetime of people to thank for my being here and being whole, and so many others who helped me write and publish this book.

Our family would not have survived without the selfless, loving help of Amy Egan, who took care of Susie when I couldn't and did so without question. Thank you for your unwavering friendship, for being "the third mom," and for believing, every step of the way, we got this.

For allowing me to discover my truth, I want to thank my partners, past and present—Audrey Buxbaum, Suzanne LaJoie, Dorothy Min, Antonette Whitehead, Leslie Gruss, and Beth Shimlock, who were steadfast and loyal through a long and painful period. And to all my DTW family, with my utmost respect, for keeping the practice going, especially Debbie Barny, Susan Nadal, and Nancy Kraus, my dear friends, who always knew what was going on and stood by me throughout.

To my friends who watched over me during this pro-

Acknowledgements

cess of recovery and believed that I would get well, my deepest gratitude. Gail Dosik, Jackie Stevens, Joey Gigliotti, Sharon Lewin, Donald Billinkoff, Susanna Weiss, Allan Lokos, Euline Blount, Deedee Vinci, Jen Lupo, Mike Visceglia, Rachel Maddow, Anne Marie Kennedy, Hendrik Helmer, Maureen Klette, Lorraine Massey, Jack Anderson, Daniel Bell, Maggie and Dean Brier, Michael Chill, Virginia Clammer, Virginia Reath, Susan Nadal, Linda Longo, Liz Goren, Rabbi Deborah Hirsch, Karen Lindsay, Alan Kurz, Sandy Russo, Robin Young, Linette John, Bonnie Shapiro, Steve Silverman, Neri Tannenbaum, Meridith Brown, Mitch Weiss, Martha Hamilton, Lauren Gerrie, Liz Albertson, Trudy Steinfeld, Joan Gondola, Steve Geller, Rena Gelman, and, sadly gone, Kathy Reback and Max Kahn.

To our knowledgeable and adept therapists—Yael Sank, Joseph Newirth, Timothy Verduin, Douglas Luce, Natalie Weder, Francheska Perepletchikova, Claire Cosentino, Elizabeth Howell, Lauralyn Fredrickson, Carl Boyer, and Marlene Steinberg—who kept our minds as healthy as possible, during the storm that was my life, somehow you all managed to keep our family together, and for that, you have my deepest gratitude.

To Susie's medical team—Deborah Axelrod, Sharon Lewin, Mihye Choi, Ruth Oratz, Arthur Ludwig, Ken Howe, Kimberly Sackheim—you have cared for Susie for the past ten years, with brilliance and love, and I cannot thank you enough.

Greatest thanks to my editor Alice Peck, who worked overtime to take a lot of pages and turn them into a book, and who got to know all of my parts and cheered them on. Bless you. It is cliché to say I couldn't have done this without you. But I guess there is a reason for clichés. And I couldn't have. Now we have a friendship for life.

Acknowledgements

To my copyeditor Ruth Mullen, who made invaluable and insightful comments and corrections, always with kindness, especially after I thought I was finished. Thank you for understanding this book and for making it so much more accessible to those who will read it.

Thank you Duane Stapp, your design of the book was intuitive and thoughtful. You generously listened to all of my suggestions and thoughts, always with my best interests at heart. Your guidance and expertise helped bring the many elements of *Brain Storm* together, and finally enabled me go to print.

To my literary agent, Steve Harris, you remained loyal and kind as you tried your damnedest to get a publisher; my best sounding board for all things literary. Thank you for believing in this book.

Wiley Saichek, my publicist—joyful and smart—you came into my life when the book was completed and had nowhere to go. You believed in *Brain Storm* and distributed it early so that it had an audience even before it was printed and for sale.

The incomparable Robin Morgan, who read the manuscript early on, gave brilliant notes and suggested that Brain Storm would be a perfect title, which, of course, it was. Your loving and beautiful introduction to this book will stay with me forever.

Heartfelt thanks to Olympia Sage Kriegel, Otis Kriegel, and Carlin Greenstein for their special contribution to the book.

All my love to our families, who did their best to understand and accept me and my diagnosis. Bob Kolton, Joanna and Andrew Schaffler, JT and Danielle Klette, Jordan Kolton, Melissa Pierce, Lisa and Rob Kirk, Bob and Anita Goldberg.

You are all blessed to now know Yael, the therapist who had the guts to

Acknowledgements

delve into the satanic world with me and save my life. No words here can really thank her enough, but I hope that this book will enable others to see her mind, her warmth, and her compassion at work.

Flannery, Lili, and Ruthie—my beautiful miracles. You loved me unconditionally during times of confusion and madness. I am blessed beyond measure for your devotion and compassion which fueled my need to heal. I thank you endlessly for having the grace and the courage to hang in there as I found my way back to motherhood.

A special thank you to Flannery. Your artistic vision in contributing to the design of the book's cover was, not surprisingly, remarkable. I have hoped, for a very long time, that someday, something would come along that we could work on together. You inspired and delighted me and I could not be happier that we were able to share this experience.

And finally to Susie, my wife, my love, my rock. You encouraged me to write. Draft after draft you read and reread the manuscript, giving me notes that only another writer could, always making it better. When I wanted to quit you made sure I kept going. You are strong, steadfast, and true. And when most would have left, you stayed. I love you forever.